The Psalms • Part III

OneBook.

DAILY–WEEKLY

The Psalms · Part III

Brian D. Russell

Printed in the United States of America

Cover design by Strange Last Name
Page design by PerfecType, Nashville, Tennessee

Russell, Brian D., 1969-
The Psalms. Part III / Brian D. Russell. – Franklin, Tennessee : Seedbed Publishing, ©2018.

pages ; cm. + 1 videodisc – (OneBook. Daily-weekly)

ISBN 9781628245783 (paperback)
ISBN 9781628245820 (DVD)
ISBN 9781628245790 (Mobi)
ISBN 9781628245806 (ePub)
ISBN 9781628245813 (uPDF)

1. Bible. Psalms -- Textbooks. 2. Bible. Psalms -- Study and teaching. 3. Bible. Commentaries. I. Title. II. Series.

BS1430.55 .R873 2018 223/.206 2016907761

SEEDBED PUBLISHING
Franklin, Tennessee
seedbed.com

CONTENTS

WELCOME TO ONEBOOK DAILY-WEEKLY

John Wesley, in a letter to one of his leaders, penned the following:

> O begin! Fix some part of every day for private exercises. You may acquire the taste which you have not: what is tedious at first, will afterwards be pleasant. Whether you like it or not, read and pray daily. It is for your life; there is no other way; else you will be a trifler all your days. . . . Do justice to your own soul; give it time and means to grow. Do not starve yourself any longer. Take up your cross and be a Christian altogether.

Rarely are our lives most shaped by our biggest ambitions and highest aspirations. Rather, our lives are most shaped, for better or for worse, by those small things we do every single day.

At Seedbed, our biggest ambition and highest aspiration is to resource the followers of Jesus to become lovers and doers of the Word of God every single day, to become people of One Book.

To that end, we have created the OneBook Daily-Weekly. First, it's important to understand what this is not: warm, fuzzy, sentimental devotions. If you engage the Daily-Weekly for any length of time, you will learn the Word of God. You will grow profoundly in your love for God, and you will become a passionate lover of people.

How Does the Daily-Weekly Work?

Daily. As the name implies, every day invites a short but substantive engagement with the Bible. Five days a week you will read a passage of Scripture followed by a short segment of teaching and closing with questions for refection and self-examination. On the sixth day, you will review and reflect on the previous five days.

Weekly. Each week, on the seventh day, find a way to gather with at least one other person doing the study. Pursue the weekly guidance for gathering. Share learning, insight, encouragement, and most important, how the Holy Spirit is working in your lives.

That's it. Depending on the length of the study, when the eight or twelve weeks are done, we will be ready with the next study. On an ongoing basis, we will release new editions of the Daily-Weekly. Over time, those who pursue this course of learning will develop a rich library of Bible learning resources for the long haul.

OneBook Daily-Weekly will develop eight- and twelve-week studies that cover the entire Old and New Testaments. Seedbed will publish new studies regularly so that an ongoing supply of group lessons will be available. All titles will remain accessible, which means they can be used in any order that fits your needs or the needs of your group.

If you are looking for a substantive study to learn Scripture through a steadfast method, look no further.

WEEK ONE

New Beginnings
Psalms 90–93

ONE
Welcome to Books IV and V of the Psalter (90–150)

Key Observation. Books IV and V of the Psalter serve as the conclusion to Scripture's prayer book for God's missional people.

Understanding the Word. Welcome to Books IV and V (90–150) of the Psalter! Book III ended with two psalms lamenting individual pain (88) and national calamity (89). In Psalm 88, an individual in deep anguish prays to the Lord but finds no relief. Psalm 89 focuses on the loss of the Davidic covenant and the forsakenness God's people experienced following the destruction of Jerusalem by the Babylonians (587 BC) and in exile to Babylon. Psalm 89:46–51 concludes with a desperate plea to the Lord for renewal.

Book III ends with God's people metaphorically in the season of winter. Individually and corporately they suffered. The good news is that winter always ends and spring returns to bring renewal. The key to leveraging spring is recognizing the opportunity and taking action. How can God's people experience renewal? What are the next steps for moving forward to the abundant future that the conclusion of the Psalter (146–150) proclaims?

Book IV answers this question by calling God's people back to their roots. David will remain an important figure, but Book IV reminds God's people of a key truth: the Lord is Israel's true King. Human leaders have authority only to the extent that they adhere faithfully to God's ways (Psalms 1, 19, 119; cf.

Deuteronomy 17:14–20 and Joshua 1:1–9). It is no coincidence that Psalm 90 bears the title, "A Prayer of Moses, the man of God."

Psalms 90–100 focus on the issue of security (cf. Psalms 46–48). These psalms proclaim the eternal kingdom of the Lord. The second part of Book IV involves a collection of hymns of praise that concludes with two psalms (105, 106) focused on Israel's history. Psalms 101–106 contain multiple recurrences of the Lord's core attribute: steadfast love/loyalty (in Hebrew, *hesed*). Israel's hope for renewal rests in the character of the Lord who is loving and merciful (Exodus 34:6–7; 1 John 4:8).

Book V builds on this foundation of security and love. It envisions new life rooted in God's faithfulness and his people's embrace of it for their present/future lives. After opening with a thanksgiving song (Psalm 107) celebrating God's loyal love (*hesed*), we will encounter three psalms attributed to David (108–110). Psalms 111–118, known traditionally as the Egyptian *Hallel* (praise), form a block of psalms celebrating Israel's foundational experience of the exodus. Psalm 119 anchors Book V and reaffirms the central role of Scripture in the life of faith (cf. Psalms 1, 19). Psalms 120–134 are the Songs of Ascent—songs used by worshippers as they travelled to the temple in Jerusalem. Psalms 135–137 interpret Israel's history by emphasizing the Lord's *hesed* (136) and memorializing the extreme anguish of the exile and loss of the temple (137). Psalms 138–145 are a final block of Davidic psalms. Thus, the Davidic psalms (108–110 and 138–145) serve as a frame around the rest of Book V.

The Psalter concludes with five psalms of exuberant praise (146–150; see Week 2 of *Psalms: Part One*). The final word for God's people and all creation will be an unending praise to the Lord for who he is and what he has done.

1. Reflect on seasons of winter in your own life. How did your faith sustain you in your most difficult challenges?

2. Books IV and V focus on the themes of security, God's love, Scripture, and God's work in history to bring salvation. How might these serve to bring you hope in our day?

TWO

Psalm 90

Psalm 90 NRSV *Lord, you have been our dwelling place in all generations. [2]Before the mountains were brought forth, or ever you had formed the earth and the world, from everlasting to everlasting you are God.*

[3]You turn us back to dust, and say, "Turn back, you mortals." [4]For a thousand years in your sight are like yesterday when it is past, or like a watch in the night.

[5]You sweep them away; they are like a dream, like grass that is renewed in the morning; [6]in the morning it flourishes and is renewed; in the evening it fades and withers.

[7]For we are consumed by your anger; by your wrath we are overwhelmed. [8]You have set our iniquities before you, our secret sins in the light of your countenance.

[9]For all our days pass away under your wrath; our years come to an end like a sigh. [10]The days of our life are seventy years, or perhaps eighty, if we are strong; even then their span is only toil and trouble; they are soon gone, and we fly away.

[11]Who considers the power of your anger? Your wrath is as great as the fear that is due you. [12]So teach us to count our days that we may gain a wise heart.

[13]Turn, O LORD! How long? Have compassion on your servants! [14]Satisfy us in the morning with your steadfast love, so that we may rejoice and be glad all our days. [15]Make us glad as many days as you have afflicted us, and as many years as we have seen evil. [16]Let your work be manifest to your servants, and your glorious power to their children. [17]Let the favor of the Lord our God be upon us, and prosper for us the work of our hands—O prosper the work of our hands!

Key Observation. In seasons of hardship, the eternal God is our hope and the source of renewal for an abundant future.

Understanding the Word. Psalm 90 is a prayer for renewal linked with Moses, the man of God. This is an important reference. Psalm 89 ended in passionate lament for deliverance, and now Psalm 90 points the way forward by focusing on the foundation for faith and hope. The rule of David and his successors had failed due to sin and disobedience. The doorway to the future is a return to the roots of faith.

Psalm 90 unfolds in three parts: verses 1–6, 7–12, and 13–17. The first section focuses on the contrast between God as the eternal Lord over creation and the finiteness of human life. Verses 1–2 ground the psalm in the relationship and security that God's people find in the Lord. This is a prayer of deep faith that recognizes that God is *our* God. This God is the powerful Creator of all that is.

In contrast, humanity is mortal. Our lives are short. God's perspective is eternal and timeless. Human days come and go. All of us recognize this by reflecting on how fast our days go by. The psalmist invites us to think about how a short human life compares with eternity. This is humbling.

Yet this psalm is not merely about the shortness of life. God's people have a deeper problem (vv. 7–12). They have experienced life under the wrath of God. The reference to days lived under wrath is a reminder of the Babylonian exile as well as the suffering of God's people under foreign rule in the years that followed their return. As we pray this psalm, we live in the hope of Jesus the Messiah, but we recognize the challenge of living faithfully in our day. These verses are pessimistic about life but they help us to frame our prayers during troubling times—be it international tensions, persecution of believers, or individual seasons of trial. Verses 11–12 add perspective. Verse 11 reminds us of the power and duration of God's anger. The purpose is not to portray God as one who is raging and eternally angry, but rather to ponder how the long days of trouble will continue. Verse 12 petitions God for an answer so that those who pray can gain wisdom and insight for living through the winters of life.

The psalmist now shows us the way forward (vv. 13–17). What is the basis for optimism and hope for the future? It is the Lord. The psalmist believes in an abundant future that will make the days of sorrow a distant past. Observe the words used to describe God's saving actions: pity/compassion (v. 13), steadfast love (v. 14), glorious power (v. 16), and favor (v. 17). When God brings renewal, his people will experience joy (v. 14), gladness (vv. 14–15), and prosperity (v. 17). As followers of Jesus who seek to share God's good news with the world, we likewise anticipate a glorious future. This new day began when Jesus announced God's kingdom (Matthew 4:17; Mark 1:14–15) and we look forward to its full manifestation in a new heaven and earth (Revelation 21). This psalm reminds us of this hope. It provides a prayer for when we find ourselves in days of darkness.

1. Reflect on times when you felt despair in your faith. How did you find your way back?
2. How does Psalm 90 challenge us to pray in times of unceasing hardship?

THREE

Psalm 91

Psalm 91 *Whoever dwells in the shelter of the Most High will rest in the shadow of the Almighty. [2]I will say of the LORD, "He is my refuge and my fortress, my God, in whom I trust."*

[3]Surely he will save you from the fowler's snare and from the deadly pestilence. [4]He will cover you with his feathers, and under his wings you will find refuge; his faithfulness will be your shield and rampart. [5]You will not fear the terror of night, nor the arrow that flies by day, [6]nor the pestilence that stalks in the darkness, nor the plague that destroys at midday. [7]A thousand may fall at your side, ten thousand at your right hand, but it will not come near you. [8]You will only observe with your eyes and see the punishment of the wicked.

[9]If you say, "The LORD is my refuge," and you make the Most High your dwelling, [10]no harm will overtake you, no disaster will come near your tent. [11]For he will command his angels concerning you to guard you in all your ways; [12]they will lift you up in their hands, so that you will not strike your foot against a stone. [13]You will tread on the lion and the cobra; you will trample the great lion and the serpent.

[14]"Because he loves me," says the LORD, "I will rescue him; I will protect him, for he acknowledges my name. [15]He will call on me, and I will answer him; I will be with him in trouble, I will deliver him and honor him. [16]With long life I will satisfy him and show him my salvation."

Key Observation. The Lord is a refuge and protector of the faithful. God has the best interest of his people in his heart.

Understanding the Word. Psalm 90 offered a prayer from Moses as a way forward for God's people in troubling times. Psalm 91 builds on this foundation by offering words to cultivate deep trust. We can pray with confidence because of who the Lord is and the security he provides. The psalmist teaches through repetition about the security found in the Lord alone.

Psalm 91 unfolds in two parts. In verses 1–13, the psalm addresses an individual believer with truths about God. In verses 14–16, the Lord himself speaks to the faithful person. Both sections emphasize the care and protection found in God.

We saw that Psalm 90 ended with a prayer for God's favor. Here we see that Psalm 91 serves to assure readers of the present reality of God's provisions. Verses 1–2 begin by declaring the security and shelter that one finds in the Lord. The imagery of shadow and shelter occurs also in Psalms 27:5, 31:20, 61:4, and 63:7. In response to God's protection, his people declare their resolute trust in him alone. To trust in the Lord is to turn from all other sources of security. These opening verses invite us to search our hearts for undivided loyalty.

Under the Lord's shelter, the faithful may live free from the common fears of humanity. Verses 3–13 provide details of the extent of the security that God provides. These verses are bold and audacious claims of protection. God's people need not fear entrapment or disease (v. 3), hostile threats (vv. 5–6), the danger posed by vastly more numerous enemies (v. 7), evil in general (v. 10), or ferocious lions and poisonous snakes (v. 13). God's people are safe because he is with them.

What do we make of these comprehensive claims of protection? In the Gospels, Satan quotes verses 11–12 during Jesus' temptation (Matthew 4:6; Luke 4:10–11). He dares Jesus to jump off the temple and allow God's angels to catch him. This is an important caution for us about biblical interpretation. Satan errs by not understanding that the promises of Psalm 91 are rooted in God's desires and plans. The life of faith does not act recklessly so as to test God's promises. Thus Jesus rejects Satan's reading.

Trust is at the heart of this psalm. It declares to us that we can trust God because he has our ultimate security and best interests in his heart. In fact, verses 14–16 add God's voice to make this point. By shifting from the psalmist's own voice to God's direct speech, these verses bring Psalm 91 to a climax. Not only can we say that God is our refuge, but he himself declares it! God's words address the faithful (those who love the Lord and acknowledge/know his name). In other words, to be faithful means that one has skin in the game. The faithful openly live and speak in a way that makes clear their allegiance. To

God's people who live faithfully and boldly, God affirms personally his unconditional commitment and accessibility to them. This is good news for us as we seek to serve as ambassadors of God's kingdom in our day.

1. How does Psalm 91 assure us of God's faithfulness in providing a refuge and security?
2. What is the mark of the faithful person in Psalm 91?

FOUR

Psalm 92

Psalm 92 ESV *It is good to give thanks to the LORD, to sing praises to your name, O Most High; [2]to declare your steadfast love in the morning, and your faithfulness by night, [3]to the music of the lute and the harp, to the melody of the lyre. [4]For you, O LORD, have made me glad by your work; at the works of your hands I sing for joy.*

[5]How great are your works, O LORD! Your thoughts are very deep! [6]The stupid man cannot know; the fool cannot understand this: [7]that though the wicked sprout like grass and all evildoers flourish, they are doomed to destruction forever; [8]but you, O LORD, are on high forever. [9]For behold, your enemies, O LORD, for behold, your enemies shall perish; all evildoers shall be scattered.

[10]But you have exalted my horn like that of the wild ox; you have poured over me fresh oil. [11]My eyes have seen the downfall of my enemies; my ears have heard the doom of my evil assailants.

[12]The righteous flourish like the palm tree and grow like a cedar in Lebanon. [13]They are planted in the house of the LORD; they flourish in the courts of our God. [14]They still bear fruit in old age; they are ever full of sap and green, [15]to declare that the LORD is upright; he is my rock, and there is no unrighteousness in him.

Key Observation. Expressing our gratitude for God's deliverance brings joy and offers a compelling hope to the faithful who hear our testimony.

Understanding the Word. Psalm 92 bears the title, "A Song for the Sabbath," and as such, it is the only psalm connected to a specific day. Sabbath is a time for reflection. It invites us back to creation and reminds us that the climactic act of creation was God's ceasing of activity on the seventh day (Genesis 2:2–3; Exodus 20:8–11). Sabbath is a reminder that God's intentions for all creation are good. His good intentions add a future-oriented dimension to Sabbath and cultivate an audacious hope that sustains us in the present. Psalm 92 captures this sentiment through its praise and thanksgiving. Following Psalm 90's lament for God's salvation and Psalm 91's assurance of God's protection, Psalm 92 reports an actual experience of deliverance. The Lord does indeed rescue his people. Seasons of hardship and winter eventually come to an end. Psalm 92 gives us a voice for celebrating such times. It also provides hope as we await our personal experience of grace.

Psalm 92 unfolds in three parts: verses 1–4, 5–11, and 12–15. Verses 1–4 announce the core intention of the psalmist. The Lord has acted so the psalmist must give thanks, sing praise, and declare the Lord's steadfast and loyal love. The purpose of a thanksgiving psalm is to make known experiences of God's saving love to the community. Gratitude is critical for faith. As Book IV begins to rebuild God's people following tremendous loss personally (Psalm 88) and nationally (Psalm 89), Psalm 92 announces that the Lord still saves people from difficult circumstances. In response, the psalmist gives thanks perpetually, "in the morning . . . by night" (v. 2). The experience of God's loyal love creates gladness and joy (v. 4; cf. Philippians 4:4–7).

In verses 5–11, the psalmist praises the Lord for his great works and deep thoughts. "Thoughts" (v. 5) refers to the plans and intentions of the Lord. Those who set themselves against God's mission and against God's people take a huge risk. Practitioners of evil will not prevail. God's enemies will perish. This is not merely a hope for vengeance. The faithful will face hardships and enemies. Living in the world as God's people can be risky. These verses remind us of the security found in the Lord regardless of the short-term success of evildoers (v. 7). The faithful must not be foolish in losing sight of this truth (v. 6). Verses 10–11 ground the psalmist's confidence in a testimony of God's deliverance. This witness to God's reversal of circumstances serves to remind his people of his reign. God rules over all creation even during the times when it seems as though evil will win.

Verses 12–15 conclude Psalm 92 with the image of a robust tree. As in Psalm 1:3, the key to the tree's robustness and ability to produce fruit is its location. Verse 13 imagines a tree planted within Jerusalem's temple. The tree's robustness and fertility serve as a living testimony to the sustaining goodness of the Lord to all who hear the psalmist's words and put their trust in God.

1. How does Psalm 92 teach us to include praise and thanksgiving in our prayers?
2. What is the purpose of the psalmist's thanksgiving?

FIVE
Psalm 93

Psalm 93 ESV *The LORD reigns; he is robed in majesty; the LORD is robed;*
he has put on strength as his belt. Yes, the world is established; it shall never be
moved. [2]*Your throne is established from of old; you are from everlasting.*
[3]*The floods have lifted up, O LORD, the floods have lifted up their voice; the*
floods lift up their roaring. [4]*Mightier than the thunders of many waters, mightier*
than the waves of the sea, the LORD on high is mighty!
[5]*Your decrees are very trustworthy; holiness befits your house, O LORD,*
forevermore.

Key Observation. The Lord's active rule over all creation is the foundation and guarantee of our security as his people.

Understanding the Word. Psalm 93 serves as an anchor. It is audacious. It orients us to a core truth that undergirds our world: the Lord reigns (v. 1, ESV or NIV) or is King (NRSV). This claim is foundational for understanding God, creation, and our life in the world. The psalmist worships the Lord as King and celebrates his eternal rule. This theme will repeat throughout Psalms 93–100. This psalm occurs in a key position in Book IV. Book III ended in individual and national tragedy (Psalms 88–89). Book IV begins, in Psalm 90, to point the way forward by sharing a lament linked with Moses. Psalms 91–92 focus on the assurance of God's protection and teach us to give thanks for God's saving ways. Psalm 93 pulls the curtain back on reality. In five short verses, this psalm declares the basis for our hope in the world and the reason that the Lord alone is worthy of our trust and praise.

Verses 1–2 announce the Lord's reign. The language is royal. God is robed in majesty and his belt is strength. God has demonstrated his power to rule by establishing order over creation (Genesis 1:1–2:3). These verses present the Lord as the true King and Ruler. The language referring to "strength as his belt" is a declaration that God continues to stand poised and ready to act decisively against any threat to creation. The Lord is firmly in control over the cosmos. God's reign is eternal. These opening verses are meant to inspire in its readers a sense of awe and recognition of our bedrock security in the King who reigns.

Verses 3–4 provide the basis for God's eternal reign. The Lord is not mere talk. He has secured the future by winning a decisive battle over a deep fear that all people experience. In ancient times, the waters of seas and rivers represented a threat to the well-being of the people. In the modern world, we still see and experience the destructive nature of water through floods, mudslides following torrential rains, hurricanes, and tsunamis. Water can create chaos and threaten life and property. In the ancient world, the floods represented anti-creation forces of evil. A deep fear that lingers today is the fear that our world may be wiped out by forces outside of the control of the average person: global warming, a plague, an asteroid strike, or a nuclear detonation. This psalm proclaims God's reign as a hedge against all forces that threaten our life and livelihood. Evil can seem formidable, but the Lord on high has defeated it in all its forms. The future is secure.

Verse 5 concludes the psalm with a return to a calm and confident picture of the Lord's rule. "Decrees" refer to the laws and statutes that God has given his people to organize and guide life—the law of the Lord (cf. Psalms 1, 19, 119). The King has secured creation and provided his people with his Word. In the New Testament, kingship finds its grounding in the life, death, and resurrection of Jesus, the Son of God. Jesus' resurrection secures his eternal kingship and provides the assurance of God's victory over all forces that threaten life.

1. What are your deepest fears in life?
2. What fears does Psalm 93 address and how does it provide an assurance of security for God's people?

WEEK ONE

GATHERING DISCUSSION OUTLINE

A. Open session in prayer. Ask that God would astonish us anew with fresh insight from God's Word and transform us into the disciples that Jesus desires us to become.

B. View the video for this week's readings.

C. What were key insights or takeaways that you gained from your reading during the week and from watching the video commentary? In particular, how did these help you to grow in your faith and understanding of Scripture this week? What parts of the Bible lesson or study raised questions for you?

D. Discuss questions selected from the daily readings.

1. **KEY OBSERVATION:** Books IV and V of the Psalter serve as the conclusion to Scripture's prayer book for God's missional people.

   DISCUSSION QUESTION: Reflect on seasons of winter in your own life. How did your faith sustain you in your most difficult challenges?

2. **KEY OBSERVATION:** In seasons of hardship, the eternal God is our hope and the source of renewal for an abundant future.

   DISCUSSION QUESTION: How does Psalm 90 challenge us to pray in times of unceasing hardship?

3. **KEY OBSERVATION:** The Lord is a refuge and protector of the faithful. God has the best interest of his people in his heart.

DISCUSSION QUESTION: How does Psalm 91 assure us of God's faithfulness in providing a refuge and security?

4. **KEY OBSERVATION:** Expressing our gratitude for God's deliverance brings joy and offers a compelling hope to the faithful who hear our testimony.

   DISCUSSION QUESTION: How does Psalm 92 teach us to include praise and thanksgiving in our prayers?

5. **KEY OBSERVATION:** The Lord's active rule over all creation is the foundation and guarantee of our security as his people.

   DISCUSSION QUESTION: What fears does Psalm 93 address and how does it provide an assurance of security for God's people?

E. As the study concludes, consider specific ways that this week's Bible lesson invites you to grow and calls you to change. How do this week's psalms teach us to pray? How do they call us to think differently? How do they challenge us to change in order to align ourselves with God's work in the world? What specific actions should we take to apply the insights of the lesson into our daily lives? What kind of person does our Bible lesson call us to become?

F. Close session with prayer. Emphasize God's ongoing work of transformation in our lives in preparation for loving mission and service in the world. Pray for missing class members as well as for persons whom we need to invite to join our study.

WEEK TWO

Security in the King

Psalms 95–99

ONE

Psalm 95

Psalm 95 *Come, let us sing for joy to the LORD; let us shout aloud to the Rock of our salvation. [2]Let us come before him with thanksgiving and extol him with music and song.*

[3]For the LORD is the great God, the great King above all gods. [4]In his hand are the depths of the earth, and the mountain peaks belong to him. [5]The sea is his, for he made it, and his hands formed the dry land.

[6]Come, let us bow down in worship, let us kneel before the LORD our Maker; [7]for he is our God and we are the people of his pasture, the flock under his care.

Today, if only you would hear his voice, [8]"Do not harden your hearts as you did at Meribah, as you did that day at Massah in the wilderness, [9]where your ancestors tested me; they tried me, though they had seen what I did. [10]For forty years I was angry with that generation; I said, 'They are a people whose hearts go astray, and they have not known my ways.' [11]So I declared on oath in my anger, 'They shall never enter my rest.'"

Key Observation. The Lord is our true King and Shepherd, so we must worship him alone and live faithfully as his people.

Understanding the Word. Building on Week One's lessons, this week's psalms (95–99) celebrate the Lord's kingship. Book IV opens with a set of psalms to help God's people chart a way forward after the disaster of exile. By centering on God's kingship and eternal reign, God's people are able to find a sure footing for moving forward as a community.

Psalm 95 has long served as a call to worship within the Christian church. The psalmist praises God as the divine King and calls his people to faithfulness by reciting the history of the exodus generation. It unfolds in two sections: an exhortation to praise (vv. 1–7c) and an exhortation to obedience (vv. 7d–11).

The psalm opens in the first-person plural as the psalmist calls on the community to join him in singing praise and thanksgiving to God (vv. 1–2). Verse 1 describes God as the rock of our salvation. This is a portrait of permanence and immovability. These are good traits for a savior.

Verses 3–5 present the reasons for praise. Verse 3 anchors worship in the Lord as the great God and King above all gods. Talk of other gods may sound strange to our ears depending on where we live and how old we are. Many of us have grown up in a culture that assumes there is only one God. Yet this was not the reality in Israel's day as God's people were surrounded by nations who did not know the Lord. Increasingly today, alternative spiritualities abound. It is relatively easy to encounter believers from most of the world religions in any major city. Observe how this psalm addresses the existence of other gods. It doesn't deny them, but simply asserts the Lord's prominence and greatness over all others. In other words, there is only one God worthy of our praise. To worship any other is to practice unfaithfulness and idolatry. Psalm 95 bases this claim in the recognition that the Lord alone is the Creator of all that is (vv. 4–5).

Verses 6–7 add a second call to worship and rationale for praise. God's people should join in worship because the Lord is "our God and we are the people of his pasture." God is no mere distant king and creator. The Lord is a shepherd who cares for his flock (Psalms 23; 77:20; 100:3). What good news!

At the end of verse 7, the psalm shifts to directly calling the congregation to hear the voice of the Lord. In verses 8–11, the Lord himself calls his people to faithful obedience, which is in contrast to the exodus generation that was disobedient in the wilderness before and after the journey from Egypt to Sinai. The stories of rebellion at Meribah and Massah (Exodus 17:1–7; Numbers 20:1–13) serve as a warning about the necessity of faithfulness. As a result of their unfaithfulness, the exodus generation did not inherit the land. As God's people, we must worship the Lord as our true King and Shepherd and serve him faithfully. In the New Testament, Jesus models faithfulness in the wilderness (Matthew 4:1–11), and Hebrews uses this psalm as the basis for its exhortation to stay true to the gospel (3:7–4:11).

1. How do the images of God as King and Shepherd impact you?
2. Why do you think that the psalmist connects the worship of God with faithfulness to his voice?

TWO

Psalm 96

Psalm 96 ESV *Oh sing to the Lord a new song; sing to the Lord, all the earth!*
2Sing to the Lord, bless his name; tell of his salvation from day to day. 3Declare
his glory among the nations, his marvelous works among all the peoples! 4For
great is the Lord, and greatly to be praised; he is to be feared above all gods. 5For
all the gods of the peoples are worthless idols, but the Lord made the heavens.
6Splendor and majesty are before him; strength and beauty are in his sanctuary.

7Ascribe to the Lord, O families of the peoples, ascribe to the Lord glory
and strength! 8Ascribe to the Lord the glory due his name; bring an offering,
and come into his courts! 9Worship the Lord in the splendor of holiness; tremble
before him, all the earth!

10Say among the nations, "The Lord reigns! Yes, the world is established; it
shall never be moved; he will judge the peoples with equity."

11Let the heavens be glad, and let the earth rejoice; let the sea roar, and all
that fills it; 12let the field exult, and everything in it! Then shall all the trees of the
forest sing for joy 13before the Lord, for he comes, for he comes to judge the earth.
He will judge the world in righteousness, and the peoples in his faithfulness.

Key Observation. The mission of God's people is to share the good news with the nations about the reign of the Lord.

Understanding the Word. Psalm 96 places God's mission front and center. It reminds all who hear it that God's kingdom is good news for the whole earth. This psalm teaches us to worship in light of the reality that God's kingdom will reign over all creation. Psalm 96 has two parts: verses 1–6 and 7–13. Both sections include a call to praise (vv. 1–3 and 7–12) followed by the rationale for worship (vv. 4–6 and 13).

The psalm begins with a threefold call to sing to the Lord (vv. 1–2). Following the warning at the end of Psalm 95, Psalm 96 invites a "new song" centered on God's mighty acts of salvation for all the earth. This song extends to the nations and reminds us of the Lord's universal reign. We are invited to pray and sing as if the future glory of God is already present. Imagine the power of singing this hymn during times of chaos and uncertainty. It also reminds us that all people will one day give the Lord the honor due his name (cf. Psalms 148–150; Philippians 2:9–11; Revelation 7:9–10). Such praise finds its roots in God's mighty acts of salvation (v. 3). For Israel, this meant focusing on the exodus (Exodus 15:11; Psalm 77:12). For Christians, we focus on God's saving actions through Jesus.

The Lord's actions communicate key truths to the world. First, God is unique in his position over all others gods (v. 4). The Lord is great and worthy of worship above all others. Second, the nations' gods are mere idols (v. 5); they wield no power. The Lord is the world's sole ruler (Psalm 95:3–5). In creation, the Lord demonstrated his power over all over deities. The trappings of true deity surround the Lord: splendor, majesty, strength, and beauty (v. 6).

Verse 7 begins the second half of the psalm. "Ascribe" is a call to bring praise and an offering to the Lord (vv. 7–8). The focus remains on all nations joining in the praise (vv. 7, 9–10). In Genesis 12:3b, God promised Abraham that all families of the earth would be blessed in him (cf. Galatians 3:8). Psalm 96 anticipates this reality and envisions the nations worshipping the Lord with God's people. Verse 10 declares the Lord's reign and roots this in God's control over the earth (cf. Psalms 93:1; 95:3; 97:1).

Verses 11–13a serve as the psalm's climax by exhorting creation itself to join in the praise (cf. Psalm 148). All creation, from the heavens and the earth and seas (v. 11) to the fields and trees (v. 12), must sing God's praises.

Verse 13b provides a glimpse of what God's reign means. There will be a day of reckoning and judgment. This is good news because God's future is one of righteousness and faithfulness. We can pray and sing this psalm in the assurance that God's future is a beautiful one. As his people, we get to be heralds and bearers of this good news to the nations, while presently praying with earnest Jesus' words: "Your kingdom come your will be done on earth as it is in heaven" (Matt. 6:10).

1. How does Psalm 96 envision our mission in the world?
2. How does this psalm provide security for us in the present?
3. How is God's future day of judgment good news for us and for the world?

THREE

Psalm 97

Psalm 97 NRSV *The LORD is king! Let the earth rejoice; let the many coastlands be glad! 2Clouds and thick darkness are all around him; righteousness and justice are the foundation of his throne. 3Fire goes before him, and consumes his adversaries on every side. 4His lightnings light up the world; the earth sees and trembles. 5The mountains melt like wax before the LORD, before the Lord of all the earth.*

6The heavens proclaim his righteousness; and all the peoples behold his glory. 7All worshipers of images are put to shame, those who make their boast in worthless idols; all gods bow down before him. 8Zion hears and is glad, and the towns of Judah rejoice, because of your judgments, O God. 9For you, O LORD, are most high over all the earth; you are exalted far above all gods.

10The LORD loves those who hate evil; he guards the lives of his faithful; he rescues them from the hand of the wicked. 11Light dawns for the righteous, and joy for the upright in heart. 12Rejoice in the LORD, O you righteous, and give thanks to his holy name!

Key Observation. The Lord rules with righteousness and justice.

Understanding the Word. Psalm 97 continues the celebration of the Lord's reign over creation. This powerful hymn unfolds in three sections: verses 1–5 are a poetic portrait of God's appearance and declaration of kingship, verses 6–9 show the response to God's kingship, and verses 10–12 tell the good news of God's kingship for his people.

The psalm opens by declaring the Lord's reign (cf. Psalms 93:1; 95:3; 96:10; 98:6; 99:1). In response, the psalmist calls the earth to worship. The focus on the whole earth in worship emphasizes the universal scope of God's authority. God's reign is sovereign over all.

Verses 2–5 shift to a rich description of the Lord's presence using storm imagery (cf. Exodus19:16–19; Habakkuk 3:2–15). God's immediate presence is described as clouds and thick darkness, consuming fire, and lightning. These images create shock and awe for all who stand before the Lord. Like Isaiah, such a powerful display of God's presence confronts us with a sense of our own ruin (Isaiah 6:5). In verses 4–5, the earth and the mountains recoil in fear and trembling. The Lord who reigns is an awe-inspiring King and this is good news. Righteousness and justice are at the center of God's rule (v. 2). In other words, the Lord's rule is not based on power alone, but on ethics. Righteousness and justice are words that describe a world of peace and fairness, a world that promotes life and good. Such a world stands in contrast to one ruled solely by might and power. The Lord's reign stands against all the forces of evil that threaten the good of this world.

What is the expected response to this dynamic vision of the Lord as King? Creation responds with an affirmation of God's righteousness. Verses 6–9 call the heavens and all peoples (v. 6), all gods (v. 7), and God's people (v. 8) to worship in recognition of the Lord. The Lord's righteousness (v. 6) and justice (v. 8; our text reads "judgments," but in Hebrew it's the same word that is translated "justice" in verse 2) are cited as reasons for this praise, in addition to the exclamation of God's rank above creation and all other gods (v. 9).

Verse 7 returns to the theme of the idolatry seen earlier in this week's study (Psalms 95:3 and 96:4–5). There is no object or being worthy of worship apart from God. The Lord is beyond comparison with any other god. In fact, the gods themselves are commanded to worship the Lord. Notice the power of this statement. We must not worship other gods because even *they* worship the Lord.

The third stanza (vv. 10–12) details the meaning of God's righteous and just reign. It addresses those whom the Lord loves (v. 10). The response for such persons is to stand against all evil in the assurance that the Lord stands with them. The psalm ends with a concluding call for rejoicing and thanksgiving to our great King.

1. How do the righteousness and justice of the Lord reveal him as distinct from all other gods and human rulers?

2. What gods in our lives do we need to turn away from in order to worship the Lord as the one "exalted far above all gods" (v. 9)?

FOUR

Psalm 98

Psalm 98 ESV *Oh sing to the Lord a new song, for he has done marvelous things! His right hand and his holy arm have worked salvation for him. [2]The Lord has made known his salvation; he has revealed his righteousness in the sight of the nations. [3]He has remembered his steadfast love and faithfulness to the house of Israel. All the ends of the earth have seen the salvation of our God.*

[4]Make a joyful noise to the Lord, all the earth; break forth into joyous song and sing praises! [5]Sing praises to the Lord with the lyre, with the lyre and the sound of melody! [6]With trumpets and the sound of the horn make a joyful noise before the King, the Lord!

[7]Let the sea roar, and all that fills it; the world and those who dwell in it! [8]Let the rivers clap their hands; let the hills sing for joy together [9]before the Lord, for he comes to judge the earth. He will judge the world with righteousness, and the peoples with equity.

Key Observation. All creation worships the Lord with joy because of his saving and just reign.

Understanding the Word. Psalm 98 resounds in praise to the Lord who saves. It captures the joy of God's people and of the whole world for the God who liberates and rules with righteousness, love, and faithfulness. In fact, this psalm was the inspiration behind Isaac Watt's familiar hymn, "Joy to the World."

Psalm 98 unfolds in two sections: verses 1–3 and 4–9. God's people are the focus of verses 1–3, where they receive the invitation to "sing a new song to the Lord" (cf. Psalm 96:1). The Lord has achieved a great victory and worked salvation for his people. The new song emphasizes the "marvelous things" that God has done (v. 1). This invites worshippers to reflect on how God's salvation has impacted their lives. The Israelites would have remembered the exodus from Egypt, the gift of the land of Canaan, and the return from Babylonian exile. The struggles of Psalms 88–89 are past. The Lord is bringing renewal to the world through a revival of his people. The words, "right hand and his holy arm" (v. 1), which are symbols of God's power, echo back to the exodus from Egypt (Exodus 15:6).

Verses 2–3 remind God's people that moments of grace from God serve as a testimony of his greatness to the rest of the world. There is always a missional dimension to the Lord's actions. Salvation is never merely about us. Good news comes to us on its way to others. The Lord is a God of love and faithfulness and his actions for Israel are ultimately actions for the world (Genesis 12:3b; Exodus 19:5–6; Isaiah 42:6 and 49:6). As God's people, we worship him now in the anticipation that *all* people will join us someday.

The second part of Psalm 98 imagines a future in which all creation joins in the praise (cf. Psalms 65–67; 148; 150). There is no mention of enemies or the forces of chaos. God's victory has been won. As followers of Jesus, we live in the anticipation of God's final victory and new creation (Revelation 21:1–5). God's mighty acts for Israel in the Old Testament and for us through Jesus' life, death, and resurrection are a foretaste of the coming of his kingdom which will be fully made manifest "on earth as it is in heaven" (Matt. 6:10).

In verses 4–6, all creation worships the Lord as its true King in exuberant song and with an array of instruments. We can imagine the terror and dread that might accompany the arrival of certain rulers and kings, but the Lord is different. When the Lord reigns, joyful praise marks the occasion.

Verses 7–9 conclude the psalm by making it clear that all creation will worship—even the roaring seas and all the creatures within them. God's reign even brings gladness to the rivers and hills. What makes the Lord's reign so different from that of other kings or even other gods? It is the Lord's character. Verse 3 reminded us of God's love and faithfulness. Verse 9 affirms that God judges with righteousness and fairness. This is a vision our world desperately needs today.

1. How does praise serve as a witness to the world according to Psalm 98?
2. How does the vision of global worship in Psalm 98 change the way you view world events today?

FIVE

Psalm 99

Psalm 99 ESV *The Lord reigns; let the peoples tremble! He sits enthroned upon the cherubim; let the earth quake!* [2]*The Lord is great in Zion; he is exalted over all the peoples.* [3]*Let them praise your great and awesome name! Holy is he!* [4]*The King in his might loves justice. You have established equity; you have executed justice and righteousness in Jacob.* [5]*Exalt the Lord our God; worship at his footstool! Holy is he!*

[6]*Moses and Aaron were among his priests, Samuel also was among those who called upon his name. They called to the Lord, and he answered them.* [7]*In the pillar of the cloud he spoke to them; they kept his testimonies and the statute that he gave them.*

[8]*O Lord our God, you answered them; you were a forgiving God to them, but an avenger of their wrongdoings.* [9]*Exalt the Lord our God, and worship at his holy mountain; for the Lord our God is holy!*

Key Observation. The Lord, who is King, offers us a relationship rooted in love and justice. We respond in faithfulness.

Understanding the Word. Psalm 99 calls for the exaltation and worship of the Lord. In verses 1–5, the psalmist focuses on God's reign. In verses 6–9, the psalmist cites the witness of Moses, Aaron, and Samuel as models for faithfulness and worship. By referring to three heroes of the faith, Psalm 99 makes concrete the reality of God's kingship for those who read and pray its words.

The psalm opens (vv. 1–3) with an exalted portrait of the Lord as King of all (cf. Psalms 93:1 and 97:1). What is the proper response to the Lord as King? In Psalm 97, we saw that it was gladness. Here, the response is awe and trembling. Verse 1 pictures God within the Holy of Holies in the Jerusalem temple. In this inner sanctum was the ark of the covenant (Exodus 25:10–17). The top cover of the ark was called the mercy seat. On each side of the ark was a cherub. The cherubim were depictions of heavenly beings who attended God in his throne room. The Lord reigns from this lofty position in Zion. Of course, the psalmist is not restricting God's presence only to the Holy of

Holies. Instead, this portrait serves as a vivid symbol of God's power over all people (v. 2).

In response, all peoples ought to praise God for his greatness and awesomeness (v. 3). Why is God worthy of global praise? It is not merely that he rules from Zion. It is because the Lord is holy. As the holy one, the Lord is the Creator, Protector, and Deliverer of his people. Because he is holy, the Lord does what is right at the right time every time. The good news of this psalm is the presence of the holy one with his people. As we read through the Bible, the presence of God with his people reaches its climax when the Word becomes flesh in Jesus (John 1:14). After Jesus' resurrection, the Holy Spirit fills believers who then become temples of God's Spirit (1 Corinthians 6:19).

Verses 4–5 remind us that the Lord is a different type of king. As the holy one, he rules with justice and righteousness. He rules as no other king ever has.

The second half of Psalm 99 reflects on God's work in history. Verse 6 recounts three models of faithfulness: Moses, Aaron, and Samuel. Each experienced a deep relationship with God. Verse 7 anchors this relationship in their faithfulness to God's instructions. The words "testimonies" and "statute" refer to the laws given to Moses at Sinai (Exodus 19:1–Num. 10:10; Deut. 5:1–28:68).

The testimony of the lives of Moses, Aaron, and Samuel is rich. God answered, forgave, and held them accountable for their missteps. Their lives affirm that God is *for* God's people. This remains true today. In response, verse 9 ends with a call to exalt the Lord as *our* God and bow in worship at his holy mountain Zion for the Lord is indeed holy (cf. v. 5)! As followers of Jesus, we find a similar call in Philippians 2:10–11: "At the name of Jesus every knee should bow and every tongue confess in heaven and on earth and under the earth that Jesus Christ is Lord to the glory of God the Father."

1. For what specific reasons does Psalm 99 teach us to worship the Lord?
2. How do Moses, Aaron, and Samuel model faithfulness in Psalm 99?

WEEK TWO

GATHERING DISCUSSION OUTLINE

A. Open session in prayer. Ask that God would astonish us anew with fresh insight from God's Word and transform us into the disciples that Jesus desires us to become.

B. View the video for this week's readings.

C. What were key insights or takeaways that you gained from your reading during the week and from watching the video commentary? In particular, how did these help you to grow in your faith and understanding of Scripture this week? What parts of the Bible lesson or study raised questions for you?

D. Discuss questions selected from the daily readings.

1. **KEY OBSERVATION:** The Lord is our true King and Shepherd, so we must worship him alone and live faithfully as his people.

   DISCUSSION QUESTION: How do the images of God as King and Shepherd impact you?

2. **KEY OBSERVATION:** The mission of God's people is to share the good news with the nations about the reign of the Lord.

   DISCUSSION QUESTION: How does Psalm 96 envision our mission in the world?

3. **KEY OBSERVATION:** The Lord rules with righteousness and justice.

DISCUSSION QUESTION: How do the righteousness and justice of the Lord reveal him as distinct from all other gods and human rulers?

4. **KEY OBSERVATION:** All creation worships the Lord with joy because of his saving and just reign.

   DISCUSSION QUESTION: How does the vision of global worship in Psalm 98 change the way you view world events today?

5. **KEY OBSERVATION:** The Lord, who is King, offers us a relationship rooted in love and justice. We respond in faithfulness.

   DISCUSSION QUESTION: How do Moses, Aaron, and Samuel model faithfulness in Psalm 99?

E. As the study concludes, consider specific ways that this week's Bible lesson invites you to grow and calls you to change. How do this week's psalms teach us to pray? How do they call us to think differently? How do they challenge us to change in order to align ourselves with God's work in the world? What specific actions should we take to apply the insights of the lesson into our daily lives? What kind of person does our Bible lesson call us to become?

F. Close session with prayer. Emphasize God's ongoing work of transformation in our lives in preparation for loving mission and service in the world. Pray for missing class members as well as for persons whom we need to invite to join our study.

WEEK THREE

Worship the King

Psalms 100, 103, 105, and 106

ONE

Psalm 100

Psalm 100 ESV *Make a joyful noise to the LORD, all the earth! [2]Serve the LORD with gladness! Come into his presence with singing!*

[3]Know that the LORD, he is God! It is he who made us, and we are his; we are his people, and the sheep of his pasture.

[4]Enter his gates with thanksgiving, and his courts with praise! Give thanks to him; bless his name!

[5]For the LORD is good; his steadfast love endures forever, and his faithfulness to all generations.

Key Observation. Worship is the central act of the people of God in response to his majestic and loving rule. It serves as a witness and invitation to the nations.

Understanding the Word. This week we will study four psalms from Book IV (100, 103, 105, and 106). Psalm 100 concludes the series of psalms that celebrate the Lord as King (93–100) by affirming key theological truths about the Lord and calling his people to worship. Psalm 103 praises the wonders of the Lord and testifies to his great love. Psalms 105 and 106 bring Book IV to a conclusion by reviewing Israel's history and envisioning a pathway forward to a future of abundance for a wayward people.

Psalm 100 is a stirring reminder of God's mission. We are worshippers who testify to the nations in word and deed about the power and love of the

Lord. In Psalms 93–99 the focus was on God's *kingship* over his people and all creation. In Psalm 100, God's people take up the missional implications of these truths. The psalm unfolds in two sections (vv. 1–3 and 4–5). Each part is similar in structure. There are a series of verbs that invite the nations to praise and worship: "Make a joyful noise," "Serve," "Come," and "Know" (vv. 1–3a), and "Enter," "Give thanks," and "bless" (v. 4). Verses 3b and 5 conclude each section respectively by providing a rationale for praise grounded in the testimony of God's people of what the Lord has done.

Verses 1–2 open with a series of invitations to worship the Lord. The emphasis is on joy and gladness. True praise of the Lord flows out of a deep relationship rooted in who God is and what God has done. Whenever praise is severed from relationship, it becomes hollow and will feel forced. As God's people, we have the privilege of praising him for the sake of the nations. Our worship tells the gospel story and calls the world to join us.

Psalm 100 imagines the nations joining God's people with exuberant praise and thanksgiving and with *service*. The word translated "serve" (v. 2) can mean "worship." It reminds us that at the heart of worship is a holistic response of committed service. It is a call to turn away from all other competing powers and gods in recognition of the true God and King, the Lord (cf. Deuteronomy 6:1–4).

Verse 3 invites the nations to *know* the Lord. This is not a call to intellectual understanding or familiarity. It is call to *allegiance*. The Lord is God in the sense that Isaiah 45:22 suggests: "I am God and there is no other." The demonstration of this truth is the existence of God's people and his ongoing care for them. God is the creator and sustainer of his people. We are not self-made. We are recipients of grace and, as such, we testify to the world.

Verses 4–5 restate these basic truths. Verse 4 envisions the nations coming to the temple in Jerusalem for worship and discovering God's people singing unto him. These songs testify to God's goodness through the years. It is a witness of God's faithful and committed love that knows no bounds.

1. How does Psalm 100 describe the meaning and purpose of worship? How is this different from your present understanding?

2. How does your life serve as a testimony to your neighbors, coworkers, and friends of God's care and compassion?

TWO

Psalm 103:1–14

Psalm 103:1–14 NRSV *Bless the Lord, O my soul, and all that is within me, bless his holy name.* [2]*Bless the Lord, O my soul, and do not forget all his benefits—*[3]*who forgives all your iniquity, who heals all your diseases,* [4]*who redeems your life from the Pit, who crowns you with steadfast love and mercy,* [5]*who satisfies you with good as long as you live so that your youth is renewed like the eagle's.*

[6]*The Lord works vindication and justice for all who are oppressed.* [7]*He made known his ways to Moses, his acts to the people of Israel.* [8]*The Lord is merciful and gracious, slow to anger and abounding in steadfast love.* [9]*He will not always accuse, nor will he keep his anger forever.* [10]*He does not deal with us according to our sins, nor repay us according to our iniquities.* [11]*For as the heavens are high above the earth, so great is his steadfast love toward those who fear him;* [12]*as far as the east is from the west, so far he removes our transgressions from us.* [13]*As a father has compassion for his children, so the Lord has compassion for those who fear him.* [14]*For he knows how we were made; he remembers that we are dust.*

Key Observation. The Lord is a healer and forgiver of sins whose love and mercy abounds for his people.

Understanding the Word. Psalm 103 reflects deeply on God's character. The psalmist praises the Lord because he is a God of steadfast love (*hesed*) and mercy/compassion. He celebrates the Lord's willingness to heal and forgive. This willingness finds its roots in the wideness and depth of God's love. Israel's story is one of grace and mercy despite their failings. This is our story too. Given the richness of this psalm, we will spend two days on it.

Psalm 103 opens with the psalmist calling on himself ("my soul") to offer praise for the lavish benefits found in the Lord (vv. 1–5). The Hebrew word translated as "soul" (*nephesh*) here refers to the totality of our being. The psalmist desires to offer his whole self (emotionally, physically, mentally, and spiritually) in witness to God's greatness. To bless the Lord's "holy name" is to recognize the implications of God's *otherness* from creation. We will return to this theme tomorrow in our discussion of verses 15–22). Verse 2 warns against forgetting the benefits of God. When we suffer and struggle, it is sometimes easier to focus on our problems rather than to remember the *abundance* of resources in the Lord.

Verses 3–5 list a series of affirmations about the Lord's actions on behalf of his people. The Lord forgives, heals, redeems, crowns, and satisfies. These are profound and personal actions. Verse 3 gives no qualification or limits to God's capacity to forgive and heal as indicated by the use of "all." This *personal* witness is the story of God's people whom he has sustained and loved despite the *national* trials of the loss of kingship and exile (Psalm 89). In fact, the Lord is capable of turning threats and chaos into restoration because of his "steadfast love and mercy" (v. 4). With the Lord, God's people will not merely survive, but live to thrive (v. 5).

Verses 6–14 describe the character of the Lord's love and mercy. Verse 6 declares God's works of vindication/righteousness and justice for "all who are oppressed." The biblical story announces a different kind of God who does not privilege the powerful and well connected. Instead the Lord is for *all*—especially those who suffer at the hands of others. This is the narrative of the history of God's people as seen in the exodus from Egypt. Verses 7–10 call to mind how God revealed himself to the Israelites at Sinai after they had built a golden calf (Exodus 32–34). Verses 8–10 allude to Exodus 34:6–7 where God shares the full meaning of his name with Moses. The Lord declared his eternal love and mercy over against the finiteness of his judgment. This was good news to God's people who had sinned greatly. It remains good news for us.

Verses 11–14 are worth memorizing. They remind God's people of what it really means that God is love. His loving mercy, compassion, and grace are without limit. This is the gospel. It is not an excuse for our sins, but it tells us that there is a way back.

1. What does it mean that God is love and what are the benefits of this love?

2. How does Psalm 103 teach us to praise and give witness to the Lord?

THREE

Psalm 103:15–22

Psalm 103:15–22 NRSV *As for mortals, their days are like grass; they flourish like a flower of the field; [16]for the wind passes over it, and it is gone, and its place knows it no more. [17]But the steadfast love of the Lord is from everlasting to everlasting on those who fear him, and his righteousness to children's children, [18]to those who keep his covenant and remember to do his commandments.*

[19]The Lord has established his throne in the heavens, and his kingdom rules over all. [20]Bless the Lord, O you his angels, you mighty ones who do his bidding, obedient to his spoken word. [21]Bless the Lord, all his hosts, his ministers that do his will. [22]Bless the Lord, all his works, in all places of his dominion. Bless the Lord, O my soul.

Key Observation. God's infinite love is our security and guide for life.

Understanding the Word. The second half of Psalm 103 (vv. 15–22) contrasts the fragility and finiteness of humanity with the infinite capacity of God's love. This theme began in verse 14 with a reference to God's remembering that "we are dust."

Verses 15–16 emphasize the transitory nature of human existence. We lack robustness and our lives are short. The comparisons with grass and flowers are vivid. They may flourish *temporarily*, but eventually they wither with the change of season and blow away with the winds of change. The psalmist's goal is not to depress us, but to cause us to see the true foundation of our security and hope.

Verses 17–18 contrast human finiteness with the reality of the Lord's steadfast love. It is eternal. It does not fade with the seasons. It is always available. In verses 17b and 18, the psalmist uses the language of fear, keeping covenant, and remembering to do his commandments to describe the human side of the relationship. This is the third time in the psalm that the fear of the Lord is mentioned. *Fear* is not a response of utter terror but of reverence. Recall that the psalmist earlier rejoiced in God's capacity to forgive sin (vv. 3 and 10–12). The Lord recognizes the imperfection of our efforts and our capacity for error (1 John 1:8–9). The risk is to think that our lives and decisions don't matter because God can and will forgive all sins. This is the wrong way to view this psalm's message. This psalm teaches us that the profound love of God is our foundation and assumes that our response will be a life of praise and faithful obedience to his ways. We practice faithfulness out of love for the God who first loved us. In other words, we fear God and practice faithfulness *because* God has loved us, forgiven us, and healed us. It is our response to his grace.

Verses 19–22 conclude this psalm with a call to worship and praise similar to verses 1–2. Verse 19 proclaims God's transcendent reign from the heavens. This is a final reminder about the radical contrast between God and us. His kingdom rules over all. This is the kingdom that Jesus announced (Matthew 4:17; Mark 1:15) and in which we serve. Verses 20–22 end with a fourfold exhortation to "bless the Lord." This call is to all creation (cf. Psalms 148 and 150), but notice the movement: beginning with the host of heaven (vv. 20–21) moving to the rest of the created order (v. 22), and finally resulting in a restatement of the psalmist's opening declaration to himself.

1. How will you respond to God's infinite love? How will this impact your daily life?
2. What is the purpose of the psalmist's contrast of God's infinite love with the finiteness of our lives? How does this reality provide hope and security for you?

FOUR

Psalm 105:1–11, 43–45

Note: Book IV ends with two historical psalms. Psalms 105 and 106 focus on two distinct portraits of Israel's history. Although both center on God's abundant grace, they offer contrasting readings. Psalm 105 is a call to praise and thanksgiving. It describes Israel's past from the perspective of God's gracious dealings with them from the calling of Abraham, Isaac, and Jacob through the exodus from Egypt and gifting of the land of Canaan. Psalm 106 is a lament that pleads for God's deliverance from exile. It likewise narrates God's acts of salvation but in the form of a confession of the inability God's people to live faithfully in response to what he has done for them. Both psalms are lengthy so we'll only read portions of each.

Psalm 105:1–11, 43–45 ESV *Oh give thanks to the Lord; call upon his name; make known his deeds among the peoples! [2]Sing to him, sing praises to him; tell of all his wondrous works! [3]Glory in his holy name; let the hearts of those who seek the Lord rejoice! [4]Seek the Lord and his strength; seek his presence continually! [5]Remember the wondrous works that he has done, his miracles, and the judgments he uttered, [6]O offspring of Abraham, his servant, children of Jacob, his chosen ones!*

[7]He is the Lord our God; his judgments are in all the earth. [8]He remembers his covenant forever, the word that he commanded, for a thousand generations, [9]the covenant that he made with Abraham, his sworn promise to Isaac, [10]which he confirmed to Jacob as a statute, to Israel as an everlasting covenant, [11]saying, "To you I will give the land of Canaan as your portion for an inheritance. . . ."

[43]So he brought his people out with joy, his chosen ones with singing. [44]And he gave them the lands of the nations, and they took possession of the fruit of the peoples' toil, [45]that they might keep his statutes and observe his laws. Praise the Lord!

Key Observation. The story of God's people serves as a testimony to the world of his faithfulness to his promises.

Understanding the Word. Psalm 105 calls on God's people to give thanks and praise to the one who promised the land of Canaan to Israel's ancestors, Abraham, Isaac, and Jacob. God delivered on this promise by liberating Israel from Egypt and guiding them into the land. This psalm is missional because it focuses on Israel being a testimony to the peoples around them (v. 1). A core principal of Scripture is this: *The gospel comes to us on its way to someone else and someplace else.* God has acted on behalf of his people for the sake of *all* peoples. God's acts of grace become the story that we share with the world about our faith. God reveals his character through saving actions in the past.

Verses 1–6 open Psalm 105 with a series of exhortations. Listen again to the string of verbs: *O give thanks . . . , call . . . , make known . . . , sing . . .* (2x), *tell . . . , glory . . . , rejoice . . . , seek . . .* (2x), and *remember.* The psalmist uses this language to call the people of God to worship. The object of their praise is the Lord, but as we've noted, this psalm has a missional dimension that is explicit from verse 1. Israel's history is a story to tell the nations.

Who is the Lord? Verses 7–11 answer this question. First, the Lord is *our* God (v. 7a). This psalm assumes a personal and community-wide commitment to the Lord. Second, God's "judgments" are made in *all the earth* (v. 7b). Third, God is faithful to his covenant promises to Israel's ancestors regarding the land of Canaan (vv. 8–11).

Psalm 105 is focused on the promised land of Canaan, which serves as the demonstration of God's faithfulness to Israel. The main body of the psalm (vv. 12–42) focuses on how God raised up Israel and delivered them repeatedly so that they could enjoy the land. The emphasis is on God's power and grace to save a people who could not have saved themselves. It is a portrait of extravagant and unmerited grace.

The conclusion (vv. 43–45) testifies that the Lord did indeed bring his people into the land and blessed them with wealth that they did not earn. The purpose of this was for witness. Verse 45 describes this witness as faithful obedience. God's people respond to his grace by reflecting his holy character through a lifestyle shaped by God's statutes and laws as revealed in the Scriptures. The psalm then ends where it began with a call to praise the Lord.

1. What are the key takeaways from Israel's history according to Psalm 105?
2. How does God's gracious work in your life give you a testimony to share with others?

FIVE

Psalm 106:1–8, 47–48

Psalm 106:1–8, 47–48 *Praise the* L*ORD.*
Give thanks to the L*ORD, for he is good; his love endures forever.*
2*Who can proclaim the mighty acts of the* L*ORD or fully declare his praise?*
3*Blessed are those who act justly, who always do what is right.*

[4]Remember me, Lord, when you show favor to your people, come to my aid when you save them, [5]that I may enjoy the prosperity of your chosen ones, that I may share in the joy of your nation and join your inheritance in giving praise.

[6]We have sinned, even as our ancestors did; we have done wrong and acted wickedly. [7]When our ancestors were in Egypt, they gave no thought to your miracles; they did not remember your many kindnesses, and they rebelled by the sea, the Red Sea. [8]Yet he saved them for his name's sake, to make his mighty power known. . . .

[47]Save us, Lord our God, and gather us from the nations, that we may give thanks to your holy name and glory in your praise.

[48]Praise be to the Lord, the God of Israel, from everlasting to everlasting.
Let all the people say, "Amen!"
Praise the Lord.

Key Observation. The grace and mercy of the Lord are greater than the sins of his people so we must turn to him in prayer.

Understanding the Word. Psalm 106 serves as a confession of Israel's inability to live faithfully. If Psalm 105 gave us a positive portrait of Israel's history, Psalm 106 details Israel's recurring failures and sins. Yet the message remains the same: *The Lord is good and his steadfast love is forever*. Psalm 106 serves as the conclusion to Book IV of the Psalter. Fittingly, it is a prayer for God's salvation and restoration from exile. Book IV has detailed the way forward for God's people. In this psalm, God's people confess their many sins across generations and open themselves up to a new work by God.

History can be sugarcoated. We can write a picture-perfect story of our lives, one that emphasizes the positive while downplaying or ignoring the negative. But if we want to go deep with God and allow him to work fully, we must let go of the pretense of looking good or viewing ourselves through rose-colored lenses. Psalm 106 serves this role for the people of God.

Verse 1 opens by calling the community to praise and give thanksgiving (cf. Psalms 105:1; 107:1). This reminds us again of the vital role that the worshipping community plays in the life of faith. Worship is the central act of God's people. We give thanks to the Lord because he is good. It may not seem like this during difficult days, but it is true. We know that God is good because of what God has done. This is the testimony of God's people throughout the ages.

Who can give thanks and praise (v. 2)? It is God's people who are loyal and faithful to him (v. 3). But verses 4–6 present a problem. Presumably the psalmist and his community are among those who "act justly" and "do what is right" (v. 3), yet they presently find themselves in need of salvation and restoration. Verse 6 cuts to the heart of the problem: "We have sinned, even as our ancestors did; we have done wrong and acted wickedly." It gets worse. From verses 7–46, the psalmist confesses the many sins of Israel's history. They have maintained a consistent pattern of unfaithfulness. Israel's rebellion can be traced all the way back to the exodus from Egypt, which was the principal act of salvation by the Lord in the Old Testament (vv. 7–8).

God's ability to save us from our sins is the heart of the gospel. "If we claim to be without sin, we deceive ourselves and the truth is not in us. If we confess our sins, he is faithful and just and will forgive us our sins and purify us from all unrighteousness" (1 John 1:8–9). In verse 47, the psalmist cries out for this salvation, so that God's people may give thanks to the Lord.

Verse 48 serves as the concluding act of praise for Book IV. God is King. God is worthy of praise. God is not finished with Israel. God will deliver anew.

1. What sins do you need to confess to the Lord today?
2. What part of your past is holding you back from becoming all that God desires for you to be?

WEEK THREE

GATHERING DISCUSSION OUTLINE

A. Open session in prayer. Ask that God would astonish us anew with fresh insight from God's Word and transform us into the disciples that Jesus desires us to become.

B. View the video for this week's readings.

C. What were key insights or takeaways that you gained from your reading during the week and from watching the video commentary? In particular, how did these help you to grow in your faith and understanding of Scripture this week? What parts of the Bible lesson or study raised questions for you?

D. Discuss questions selected from the daily readings.

1. **KEY OBSERVATION:** Worship is the central act of the people of God in response to his majestic and loving rule. It serves as a witness and invitation to the nations.

   DISCUSSION QUESTION: How does Psalm 100 describe the meaning and purpose of worship? How is this different from your present understanding?

2. **KEY OBSERVATION:** The Lord is a healer and forgiver of sins whose love and mercy abounds for his people.

   DISCUSSION QUESTION: What does it mean that God is love and what are the benefits of this love?

3. **KEY OBSERVATION:** God's infinite love is our security and guide for life.

   DISCUSSION QUESTION: How will you respond to God's infinite love? How will this impact your daily life?

4. **KEY OBSERVATION:** The story of God's people serves as a testimony to the world of his faithfulness to his promises.

   DISCUSSION QUESTION: How does God's gracious work in your life give you a testimony to share with others?

5. **KEY OBSERVATION:** The grace and mercy of the Lord are greater than the sins of his people, so we must turn to him in prayer.

   DISCUSSION QUESTION: What part of your past is holding you back from becoming all that God desires for you to be?

E. As the study concludes, consider specific ways that this week's Bible lesson invites you to grow and calls you to change. How do this week's psalms teach us to pray? How do they call us to think differently? How do they challenge us to change in order to align ourselves with God's work in the world? What specific actions should we take to apply the insights of the lesson into our daily lives? What kind of person does our Bible lesson call us to become?

F. Close session with prayer. Emphasize God's ongoing work of transformation in our lives in preparation for loving mission and service in the world. Pray for missing class members as well as for persons whom we need to invite to join our study.

WEEK FOUR

Remembering Our Roots: God's Saving Actions and Their Meaning

Psalms 107, 110–114

Psalm 107 begins the final book of the Psalter (Book V). Book IV answered this question: How can God's people move forward after the personal and national devastation of the failure of Israel's kings and the exile to Babylon? The psalms in Book IV realigned God's people with the truth that the Lord is King and our source of security. Book V builds on this by celebrating the Lord's loyal and steadfast love (*hesed*), reorienting God's people to the roots of their faith, and anticipating a final vision in which all creation will praise the Lord (Psalms 146–150). Psalm 107 reviews God's past faithfulness to his people. Psalm 110 is a royal psalm that points to Jesus. Psalms 111 and 112 offer portraits of God's work and the character of those who fear. Psalms 113 and 114 are the first two psalms of the Egyptian Hallel (113–118), which celebrate the exodus.

ONE

Psalm 107:1–3, 33–43

Psalm 107:1–3, 33–43 NRSV *O give thanks to the Lord, for he is good; for*
his steadfast love endures forever. [2]*Let the redeemed of the Lord say so, those he*
redeemed from trouble, [3]*and gathered in from the lands, from the east and from*
the west, from the north and from the south. . . .

[33]*He turns rivers into a desert, springs of water into thirsty ground,* [34]*a fruitful*
land into a salty waste, because of the wickedness of its inhabitants. [35]*He turns a*
desert into pools of water, a parched land into springs of water. [36]*And there he lets*

the hungry live, and they establish a town to live in; [37]they sow fields, and plant vineyards, and get a fruitful yield. [38]By his blessing they multiply greatly, and he does not let their cattle decrease.

[39]When they are diminished and brought low through oppression, trouble, and sorrow, [40]he pours contempt on princes and makes them wander in trackless wastes; [41]but he raises up the needy out of distress, and makes their families like flocks. [42]The upright see it and are glad; and all wickedness stops its mouth. [43]Let those who are wise give heed to these things, and consider the steadfast love of the LORD.

Key Observation. We prepare ourselves for an abundant future with God by expressing gratitude for how he has worked in our lives in the past.

Understanding the Word. Psalm 107 is a thanksgiving psalm that rejoices in the dynamic power of the Lord's steadfast loyal love (*hesed).* His love is forever without end. This is the good news that the psalmist shares. It was good news for God's people as they recovered from exile and it remains so today.

Psalm 107:1 opens with an exhortation to the community to give thanks to God for his eternal and steadfast love. Gratitude is critical for the life of faith. It is a doorway to a dynamic and secure relationship with God. When we learn to give thanks in the present, the *past* changes the meaning it has for our lives. Painful memories may remain, but their meaning changes. We become free to live fully for the Lord *now* in anticipation of an abundant future. God's people in the Old Testament were keenly aware of his lovingkindness in restoring them from exile to Babylon (vv. 2–3). Psalm 107 gives thanks from the perspective of having returned to the land. As Christians, we root our thanksgiving in the lavish love of God shown at the cross of Jesus Christ (Romans 5:8).

The middle section of the psalm (not included in the reading) describes four examples of persons whom the Lord rescued. Verses 4–9 recall God's provision of food and water to those struggling in the wilderness. Verses 10–16 narrate God's liberation of prisoners. Verses 17–22 tell how the Lord healed the sick. Verses 23–32 celebrate God's rescue of those caught in a stormy sea. Here we find tangible examples that testify to the greatness of the Lord's steadfast love (*hesed*). These verses invite us to reflect on specific ways that God has redeemed us.

Verses 33–43 bring the thanksgiving to a climax by celebrating the people's return to the land, as well as God's ability to restore it to a place of abundance. The language of these verses ties back to the four examples found in verses 4–32. The psalmist's goal is to help us learn that God's work is all around us. God delivered in the past, he delivers in the present, and he will deliver in the future. For this, we must give thanks. Verses 42–43 conclude the psalm with advice for the wise—God's people with eyes to see God's hand. We live by the grace of God. Find security in this truth and live for the Lord today.

1. How does Psalm 107 inspire you to give thanks today?
2. Why is the practice of gratitude important for the life of faith and what is its role in your life?

TWO

Psalm 110

Psalm 110 ESV *The Lord says to my Lord: "Sit at my right hand, until I make your enemies your footstool."*

*2The Lord sends forth from Zion your mighty scepter. Rule in the midst of
your enemies! 3Your people will offer themselves freely on the day of your power,
in holy garments; from the womb of the morning, the dew of your youth will
be yours. 4The Lord has sworn and will not change his mind, "You are a priest
forever after the order of Melchizedek."*

*5The Lord is at your right hand; he will shatter kings on the day of his wrath.
6He will execute judgment among the nations, filling them with corpses; he will
shatter chiefs over the wide earth. 7He will drink from the brook by the way;
therefore he will lift up his head.*

Key Observation. The Messiah secures the future for God's people and reigns forever in God's kingdom.

Understanding the Word. Psalm 110 is royal psalm celebrating the triumphant reign of Israel's king. To understand this psalm we need to remember that the book of Psalms is a product of the post-exilic period. Israel no longer had a king. Previous psalms about kingship (e.g., 2, 18, 20, 110) take on a new role. They become prayers of expectation and longing for the Messiah through whom God will usher in his kingdom (cf. Psalm 2). Psalm 89 announced the failure of the Davidic kings, and now Psalm 110 announces the new hope of a coming king who will bring security. Its words audaciously express Israel's longing for God's kingdom and liberation from the nations who oppressed them. For Christians, Psalm 110 serves prophetically to announce the coming of Jesus as King and Priest for God's people. A messianic reading of Psalm 110 has deep roots in the church. Verse 1 is quoted in the New Testament more frequently than any other Old Testament text (Matthew 22:44; Mark 14:62, 16:19; Luke 22:69; Acts 2:34–35; 7:55; Romans 8:34; Ephesians 1:20; Colossians 3:1; Hebrews 1:3, 13; 8:1; 10:12; 1 Peter 3:22).

The psalm opens with language similar to how Israel's prophets spoke. It declares that the Messiah will reign from the right hand of God's throne (v. 1). The church has consistently understood this to be a statement about King Jesus, Israel's Messiah. The foundation for this reading rests on the reference to David in the title and the language, "The LORD says to my Lord." Who would David's lord be? It would be someone even greater than he—indeed, the coming Messiah who would liberate God's people from their enemies and inaugurate the kingdom of God.

Verses 1–3 contain imagery used throughout the ancient world for kings. Verse 2 reminds God's people of the importance of Zion (cf. Psalms 46 and 48), which represented the earthly center of God's reign. These verses portray a powerful figure who will rule over all of his foes and guide his people to victory.

In the second half of Psalm 110, we see that the Messiah will have two roles: King and Priest. The political and spiritual realms often merged in the ancient world. However, in the Old Testament, though David and Solomon were instrumental in centralizing the role of Jerusalem/Zion, the offices of priest and king were usually kept separate. David brought the ark to Jerusalem (2 Samuel 6), and Solomon built the Lord's temple (1 Kings 6–8). Otherwise, the duties of king (Deuteronomy 17:14–20) and priest (Leviticus 1–7, 21; Deuteronomy 18:1–8) remained distinct. Psalm 110 celebrates the coming Messiah who will combine these roles as both the Son of David and the true High Priest. The language in verses 5–7 (similar to verses 2–3) contains standard imagery from the times for portraying a victorious king. These verses point us toward Jesus Christ's final victory at the new creation (Revelation 21) and remind us to pray, "Your kingdom come, your will be done" (Matthew 6:10) and "Come, Lord Jesus" (Revelation 22:20).

1. How does Psalm 110 teach us to pray about God's kingdom?
2. How does Psalm 110 enhance your understanding and appreciation of Jesus the Messiah?

THREE

Psalms 111 and 112

Psalms 111 and 112 are both acrostic poems. This means that in the original Hebrew the first letter of the first word in each line begins with the successive letters of the Hebrew alphabet. Psalm 111 focuses on the mighty acts of the Lord, and Psalm 112 reviews the attributes and actions of the righteous who worship the Lord.

Psalm 111 *Praise the LORD.*

I will extol the LORD with all my heart in the council of the upright and in the assembly.

[2]Great are the works of the LORD; they are pondered by all who delight in them. [3]Glorious and majestic are his deeds, and his righteousness endures forever. [4]He has caused his wonders to be remembered; the LORD is gracious and compassionate. [5]He provides food for those who fear him; he remembers his covenant forever.

[6]He has shown his people the power of his works, giving them the lands of other nations. [7]The works of his hands are faithful and just; all his precepts are trustworthy. [8]They are established for ever and ever, enacted in faithfulness and uprightness. [9]He provided redemption for his people; he ordained his covenant forever—holy and awesome is his name.

[10]The fear of the LORD is the beginning of wisdom; all who follow his precepts have good understanding. To him belongs eternal praise.

Psalm 112 *Praise the LORD.*

Blessed are those who fear the LORD, who find great delight in his commands.

[2]Their children will be mighty in the land; the generation of the upright will be blessed. [3]Wealth and riches are in their houses, and their righteousness endures forever. [4]Even in darkness light dawns for the upright, for those who are gracious

and compassionate and righteous. [5]*Good will come to those who are generous and lend freely, who conduct their affairs with justice.*

[6]*Surely the righteous will never be shaken; they will be remembered forever.* [7]*They will have no fear of bad news; their hearts are steadfast, trusting in the* Lord. [8]*Their hearts are secure, they will have no fear; in the end they will look in triumph on their foes.* [9]*They have freely scattered their gifts to the poor, their righteousness endures forever; their horn will be lifted high in honor.*

[10]*The wicked will see and be vexed, they will gnash their teeth and waste away; the longings of the wicked will come to nothing.*

Key Observation. A transformed human life is the ultimate praise for our gracious and mighty Lord and Savior.

Understanding the Word. The early church leader Irenaeus wrote, "God is given glory by a human being fully alive."[1] Psalms 111–112 testify to the truth of this statement. These two psalms teach us the greatness of God and the profound work that God can do in the life of a human being.

Psalm 111 is a hymn of praise and thanksgiving that roots worship in the remembrance of God's deeds of salvation in the exodus, wilderness, gift of the promised land, and covenant (vv. 2–9). These acts of God flow out of his core character of graciousness and compassion (v. 4b). God acts for his people *because* he is gracious and compassionate, not because God's people earn his favor. This is the heart of the gospel. Thus, Psalm 111 begins with the psalmist and the gathered community praising the Lord (v. 1).

Psalm 111 also focuses on the authoritative instructions provided through the covenant and its precepts (vv. 7–8). The psalm then assumes a response by God's people. Part of this response is *praise* itself, but the holy and awesome God who saves his people and crafts a covenant with them desires a person's *whole* life. Verse 10 hints at this and serves as a transition to Psalm 112. It echoes Proverbs 1:7, "The fear of the Lord is the beginning of knowledge, but fools despise wisdom and instruction." This truth is critical. Psalm 111 clearly calls us to praise the Lord in recognition of his character and actions. But knowing God's ways must also include personal transformation. A wise

1. *Against Heresies* IV 20.7

life is one that embraces and reflects God's character in response to our experience of grace.

What does such a life look like? Psalm 112 lays it out plainly. It begins with praise (v. 1). It is correct to praise God for the profound work that he can do in the life of an individual person (cf. Psalms 8 and 15). As in Psalm 1 (vv. 1–2, 4, 6), Psalm 112 describes the profound differences in outcomes enjoyed by the righteous and the wicked (vv. 1, 10). The language is rich. Verse 4 includes three of the attributes used of the Lord in Psalm 111—graciousness (v. 4), compassion (v. 4), and righteousness (v. 3). In other words, the person who fears the Lord witnesses to God's character through his or her life. The happy person delights in God's commandments (Psalm 1:2).

1. What is the relationship between God's character and deeds and how we live our lives?
2. In what areas of your life could you more faithfully point to God?

FOUR

Psalm 113

Psalm 113 ESV *Praise the Lord! Praise, O servants of the Lord, praise the name of the Lord!*

2Blessed be the name of the Lord from this time forth and forevermore!
3From the rising of the sun to its setting, the name of the Lord is to be praised!

4The Lord is high above all nations, and his glory above the heavens! 5Who
is like the Lord our God, who is seated on high, 6who looks far down on the
heavens and the earth? 7He raises the poor from the dust and lifts the needy
from the ash heap, 8to make them sit with princes, with the princes of his people.
9He gives the barren woman a home, making her the joyous mother of children.
Praise the Lord!

Key Observation. God displays his power and majesty by saving those who are desperate for what only he can do.

Understanding the Word. Psalm 113 is the first of a series of psalms known as the Egyptian Hallel (113–118). *Hallel* is a Hebrew word that means "praise."

These psalms served as songs of worship for God's people during Passover, as they commemorated the exodus. As Christians, the Hallel psalms help us to remember the fullest expression of God's salvation in the life, death, and resurrection of Jesus. Jesus was arrested after sharing the Passover meal with his disciples. It is possible that these were the very psalms they sang during their meal together (Matthew 26:30; Mark 14:26).

Psalm 113 is a sublime vision of the God who we worship. The power of this hymn is in the contrasts of expectation that it provides. The psalm's declaration of the Lord's greatness runs counter to the ways of the world. God's greatness manifests through God's concern for the marginalized. It witnesses to the hope that we can find in the God who loves us.

The first half of Psalm 113 offers a compelling portrait of God's awesomeness and calls his people to praise. By exhorting praise of the Lord's name (v. 1–3), the psalmist invites worshippers to reflect on the nature and character of the Lord. Who is the Lord in his essence? Verse 4 begins to answer this question by declaring the Lord's transcendence. Transcendence refers to the position and separateness of the Lord apart from the created universe. Verse 4 describes this is spatial terms. The Lord is so awesome that he exists not only "high above all nations," but also his glory is "[high] above the heavens." In other words, God exists outside of creation. This imagery highlights God's sovereignty and power. Nothing in creation can be compared to God.

The second half of Psalm 113 opens with a question: "Who is like the Lord our God?" (vv. 5–6). These verses reaffirm God's positional power and transcendence. But unlike typical expressions of power that we witness in our world, the Lord's power manifests itself on behalf of the poor and marginalized. In our world, the powerful tend to associate with persons of like status in order to accumulate more power and prestige. In contrast, the Lord is self-giving and acts *within our world* in order to extend blessing and salvation for those most desperate for what only he can do. In other words, our transcendent God is also an immanent God. God exists outside and above creation but actively moves and works *within creation* and most importantly *within our lives*.

Psalm 113 ends with portraits of God's blessing on the poor and on a woman unable to bear children. These were marginalized persons in the ancient world. Yet the God of the Bible bypasses the powerful and blesses these people in order to reverse their circumstances. This is the gospel story as well. Although Jesus was God, he humbled himself and took up the cross to give us true life (Philippians 2:6–8). How do we respond to such a portrait of God? Verse 9 reminds us, "Praise the Lord!"

1. How does the portrait of God in Psalm 113 challenge our world's ways of understanding power and greatness?
2. If Psalm 113 indeed describes how God acts, what are some specific actions we can take this week to live out God's character?

FIVE

Psalm 114

Psalm 114 NRSV *When Israel went out from Egypt, the house of Jacob from a people of strange language, [2]Judah became God's sanctuary, Israel his dominion.*

[3]The sea looked and fled; Jordan turned back. [4]The mountains skipped like rams, the hills like lambs.

[5]Why is it, O sea, that you flee? O Jordan, that you turn back? [6]O mountains, that you skip like rams? O hills, like lambs?

[7]Tremble, O earth, at the presence of the Lord, at the presence of the God of Jacob, [8]who turns the rock into a pool of water, the flint into a spring of water.

Key Observation. The exodus from Egypt and gift of the promised land are God's testimony that human power and injustice will never have the final word.

Understanding the Word. Psalm 114 is the second of the Egyptian Hallel psalms and celebrates the exodus as the heart of Israel's gospel. The Lord's deliverance of his people from Egypt and provision of a new land served as the foundational core of Israel's life with God. As followers of Jesus, we read this psalm as a celebration of the climactic acts of God's salvation in Jesus' death and resurrection. Psalm 113 presented a dramatic portrait of our awesome and transcendent Lord who acts immanently in our world on behalf of the poor and marginalized. In this psalm, we see how God did for an enslaved people what no other god has ever done. The exodus is the divine testimony that human power and injustice will never be the final word.

Psalm 114 has two parts. First, it offers a poetic portrait of the exodus, the crossings of the Red Sea and Jordan River, and Israel/Judah serving as the centerpiece of God's earthly reign (vv. 1–4). Second, it portrays the response of creation and the nations to God's demonstration of grace and power for his people (vv. 5–8).

Our faith rests on the claim that God has acted powerfully in history to save humanity. For Israel, this centered on the Lord's deliverance of his people from Egyptian slavery (Exodus 20:2). Psalm 114 reminds God's people of their deliverance from Egypt, as well as their elevation from slaves of Pharaoh to free people who lived in God's sanctuary (vv. 1–2). Verses 3–4 testify to God's mastery over the Red Sea (Exodus 14:1–15:21) and the Jordan River (Joshua 3–4). Ancient people feared the waters and understood seas and rivers as symbols of death and chaos. When the Lord made pathways through the Red Sea and Jordan River, he demonstrated his power over the forces that oppress all people. These miracles testified to the unique power of God and guaranteed the future of God's people. For Christians, Jesus' death during the Passover celebration marked it a new exodus; his resurrection announced God's ultimate victory over sin and death as God's show of power at the sea announced God's victory over Egypt. Thus, Psalm 114 invites us to reflect on how God has worked salvation for us first through the exodus and now through the life, death, and resurrection of Jesus.

Verses 5–8 describe the implications of God's mighty acts of salvation for the world. Verses 5–6 ask rhetorical questions regarding God's authority over creation. These questions beg us to respond, "Because of the Lord's awesome power and mastery over all forces that resist God's loving and just rule!" The Lord has acted on behalf of his people. How then should all others respond? Verse 7 calls for the earth to "tremble." God has acted for the weak and lowly (Psalm 113:7–9) by saving them from oppression in Egypt. The powerful will indeed tremble before the Lord's awesome power. Yet, in verse 8, we see God's kindness to Israel in the wilderness, where he provided them with water from a rock. In other words, God is gracious to those who recognize their dependence on him. Psalm 114 thus functions missionally as a witness to the nations of the power *and* grace of God.

1. What does Psalm 114 teach us about the foundation of our faith?
2. What is the significance mentioning the rest of the earth in Psalm 114:7?

WEEK FOUR

GATHERING DISCUSSION OUTLINE

A. Open session in prayer. Ask that God would astonish us anew with fresh insight from God's Word and transform us into the disciples that Jesus desires us to become.

B. View the video for this week's readings.

C. What were key insights or takeaways that you gained from your reading during the week and from watching the video commentary? In particular, how did these help you to grow in your faith and understanding of Scripture this week? What parts of the Bible lesson or study raised questions for you?

D. Discuss questions selected from the daily readings.

1. **KEY OBSERVATION:** We prepare ourselves for an abundant future with God by expressing gratitude for how he has worked in our lives in the past.

   DISCUSSION QUESTION: Why is the practice of gratitude important for the life of faith and what is its role in your life?

2. **KEY OBSERVATION:** The Messiah secures the future for God's people and reigns forever over God's kingdom.

   DISCUSSION QUESTION: How does Psalm 110 enhance your understanding and appreciation of Jesus the Messiah?

3. **KEY OBSERVATION:** A transformed human life is the ultimate praise for our gracious and mighty Lord and Savior.

   DISCUSSION QUESTION: What is the relationship between God's character and deeds and how we live our lives?

4. **KEY OBSERVATION:** God displays his power and majesty by saving those who are desperate for what only he can do.

   DISCUSSION QUESTION: How does the portrait of God in Psalm 113 challenge our world's ways of understanding power and greatness?

5. **KEY OBSERVATION:** The exodus from Egypt and gift of the promised land are God's testimony that human power and injustice will never have the final word.

   DISCUSSION QUESTION: What does Psalm 114 teach us about the foundation of our faith?

E. As the study concludes, consider specific ways that this week's Bible lesson invites you to grow and calls you to change. How do this week's psalms teach us to pray? How do they call us to think differently? How do they challenge us to change in order to align ourselves with God's work in the world? What specific actions should we take to apply the insights of the lesson into our daily lives? What kind of person does our Bible lesson call us to become?

F. Close session with prayer. Emphasize God's ongoing work of transformation in our lives in preparation for loving mission and service in the world. Pray for missing class members as well as for persons whom we need to invite to join our study.

WEEK FIVE

Remembering Our Roots II: Exodus, King, and Torah

Psalms 118 and 119

This week, we reflect on the roots of our life of faith: the exodus, Israel's Messiah, and Scripture. Psalms 118 and 119 unite king and Torah for a third time in the Psalter (Psalms 1, 2, 18, 19). Psalm 118 also reflects on the exodus as the foundation for future victories by the King.

Psalm 118, the last of the Egyptian Hallel psalms (113–118), is a thanksgiving song. It tells the story of an unexpected victory by God. Unsurprisingly, the exodus plays a prominent role in the story. The psalmist uses references to the victory song in Exodus 15:1–18 to describe the deliverance. Given its prominent use in the New Testament, we will spend two lessons on Psalm 118. Today will explore the first twenty-one verses.

ONE

Psalm 118:1–21

Psalm 118:1–21 ESV *Oh give thanks to the Lord, for he is good; for his steadfast love endures forever!*

2 *Let Israel say, "His steadfast love endures forever."* 3 *Let the house of Aaron
say, "His steadfast love endures forever."* 4 *Let those who fear the Lord say, "His
steadfast love endures forever."*

5 *Out of my distress I called on the Lord; the Lord answered me and set me
free.* 6 *The Lord is on my side; I will not fear. What can man do to me?* 7 *The Lord
is on my side as my helper; I shall look in triumph on those who hate me.*

8 *It is better to take refuge in the Lord than to trust in man.* 9 *It is better to
take refuge in the Lord than to trust in princes.*

10 All nations surrounded me; in the name of the Lord *I cut them off! 11 They surrounded me, surrounded me on every side; in the name of the* Lord *I cut them off! 12 They surrounded me like bees; they went out like a fire among thorns; in the name of the* Lord *I cut them off! 13 I was pushed hard, so that I was falling, but the* Lord *helped me.*

14 The Lord *is my strength and my song; he has become my salvation. 15 Glad songs of salvation are in the tents of the righteous: "The right hand of the* Lord *does valiantly, 16 the right hand of the* Lord *exalts, the right hand of the* Lord *does valiantly!"*

17 I shall not die, but I shall live, and recount the deeds of the Lord. *18 The* Lord *has disciplined me severely, but he has not given me over to death.*

19 Open to me the gates of righteousness, that I may enter through them and give thanks to the Lord. *20 This is the gate of the* Lord; *the righteous shall enter through it. 21 I thank you that you have answered me and have become my salvation.*

Key Observation. Thanksgiving is rooted in the loving character of God, who moves to save us in the present just as he did in the past.

Understanding the Word. Psalm 118 is one of the key psalms in the Psalter due to its heavy use by New Testament writers who quoted frequently from the second half of the psalm (vv. 22ff). They saw in the testimony of the king a foreshadowing of Jesus' overcoming of the grave through resurrection.

Psalm 118 opens with a call to God's people to give thanks (vv. 1–4). Gratitude is central to faith. Thanksgiving flows in response to God's saving work in our lives. The Lord is good and therefore deserves thanksgiving. His goodness is displayed in his eternal loving faithfulness (*hesed*). Verses 2–4 emphasize the corporate nature of this grateful celebration. All God's people participate.

In verses 5–13, the psalmist narrates a king's victory against overwhelming odds. The king fights for God's people against the forces of the nations (v. 10). It is clear that the odds of defeat were high (v. 5), but the king resolutely chose to trust in the power of the Lord. Virtually every verse affirms this choice. It was folly even to consider another source of help (vv. 6–9). The Lord is his *refuge* (v. 8; cf. Psalm 46:1) and *helper* (v. 7; cf. Psalm 121:2). These words signify security from the chaos of the world. The Lord is an ever-present guardian and sentinel. Instead of experiencing defeat (vv. 10–13), the king was victorious *because* of the Lord.

Verses 14–21 interpret the king's victory through the lens of the exodus from Egypt. As we've learned, the exodus was the central act of the Lord's salvation in the Old Testament. It defined the identity of God's people (Exodus 20:2). Psalm 118 recounts the king's victory in the context of the exodus through a series of quotations and allusions to the victory song in Exodus 15:1b–18. Verses 14 and 21 draw from Exodus 15:2. The language of God's powerful right hand (vv. 15–16) look back to Exodus 15:6.

Once the king has prevailed, he approaches the temple gates and requests admission in order to testify (vv. 19–21). When God acts, we respond with thanksgiving and praise.

As followers of Jesus, we likewise will face trying circumstances, but the power of the cross and resurrection remain for us to experience strength and renewal in our days. As the writer to the Hebrews wrote, "Jesus Christ is the same yesterday and today and forever" (13:8). In tomorrow's lesson, we will see how the final verses of Psalm 118 connect this thanksgiving psalm directly with Jesus' victory over death.

1. What is the basis for your thanksgiving to the Lord today?
2. What are your favorite words or phrases for giving thanks to God? What are the sources of these words or phrases?

TWO

Psalm 118:22–29

Today we complete our study of Psalm 118 by focusing on its concluding verses in which the community celebrates the king's victory.

Psalm 118:22–29 ESV *The stone that the builders rejected has become the*
cornerstone. [23]*This is the* L*ORD's doing; it is marvelous in our eyes.* [24]*This is the*
day that the L*ORD has made; let us rejoice and be glad in it.*

[25]*Save us, we pray, O* L*ORD! O* L*ORD, we pray, give us success!*

[26]Blessed is he who comes in the name of the LORD! We bless you from the house of the LORD. [27]The LORD is God, and he has made his light to shine upon us. Bind the festal sacrifice with cords, up to the horns of the altar!

[28]You are my God, and I will give thanks to you; you are my God; I will extol you. [29]Oh give thanks to the LORD, for he is good; for his steadfast love endures forever!

Key Observation. God's victory in the death and resurrection of Jesus is the grounds for celebration and the guarantee of salvation and an abundant future.

Understanding the Word. Psalm 118 links the saving story of the Messiah to Jesus Christ. Verse 22 is quoted repeatedly in the New Testament (Matthew 21:42; Mark 12:10; Luke 20:17; Acts 4:11; 1 Peter 2:7). This indicates that Christians understood the royal, victorious figure in Psalm 118 to be Jesus. His death on the cross and resurrection on the third day embodied the reversal from humiliation to exaltation that we find in Psalm 118.

In verses 5–18, we saw the Lord's deliverance of the king from his enemies, framed in the language of the exodus. In verses 19–21, the king arrived at the temple and requested admittance. Now, in verses 22–27, we witness the gathered community of God's people celebrate extravagantly the king's victory, which has secured a new future against the odds. This is the meaning of verse 22: the Lord won an unexpected victory, and now the king stands exalted. Christians understand Jesus' death and resurrection through the lens of Psalm 118. He is, in fact, the "stone that the builders rejected" who "has become the cornerstone" (v. 22). Verses 23–24 provide language to celebrate Jesus' resurrection, but also for those times when we know without a doubt that we prevailed *only* because of God's love, mercy, and grace.

Verses 25–27 show the response of the gathered people of God to the arrival of the king. They recognized that God had acted and they cried out in expectation that he would continue to work salvation for them. This is an important reminder about the power of thanksgiving in our lives. When we hear the testimony of God's work in another's life, we gain hope that God is able to do likewise for us.

We later hear the echoes of verses 25–26 when the crowds greeted Jesus with cheers when he entered Jerusalem (Matthew 21:9; Mark 11:9–10; Luke 19:38; John 12:13). This captures their anticipation of Jesus becoming king. The gospel, however, adds another plot twist. Jesus indeed was to become a victorious king, but first he had to live out the narrative of Psalm 118. Jesus was victorious not through the typical human means of victory—cunning and overwhelming force. Jesus was *unexpectedly* victorious by submitting to death on a cross and then rendering the power of death impotent through the resurrection. In this way, he truly fulfilled the prophetic words of Psalm 118:22 and secured the foundation for our life in this world.

The psalm ends with the victorious king proclaiming his loyalty and giving thanks and praise to the Lord (v. 28). The language is drawn from Exodus 15:2b, adding a final point of connection to the exodus. The congregation affirms the king's words by repeating the opening line of the psalm: "Oh give thanks to the LORD, for he is good; for his steadfast love endures forever" (v. 29; cf. v. 1).

1. How does Psalm 118:22–29 enhance our understanding of Jesus' death and resurrection? How does this help us to celebrate God's saving work?
2. What is the significance of the way God's people responded to the king's testimony?

THREE

Psalm 119:1–8

Psalm 119:1–8 NRSV *Happy are those whose way is blameless, who walk in the law of the LORD. [2]Happy are those who keep his decrees, who seek him with their whole heart, [3]who also do no wrong, but walk in his ways. [4]You have commanded your precepts to be kept diligently. [5]O that my ways may be steadfast in keeping your statutes! [6]Then I shall not be put to shame, having my eyes fixed on all your commandments. [7]I will praise you with an upright heart, when I learn your righteous ordinances. [8]I will observe your statutes; do not utterly forsake me.*

Key Observation. Scripture is God's authoritative instruction to guide the faithful through life.

Understanding the Word. Psalm 119 is the longest in the Psalter. It centers on the law (*torah*) of the Lord, and is the last of the Torah psalms (1, 19, and 119).

These psalms are foundational in orienting us to a life of faithfulness (1 and 19) and then reorienting us into renewed faithfulness (119) as we come to grips with our history.

Psalm 119 falls between the Egyptian Hallel psalms (113–118), which reminded God's people of the exodus, and the Songs of Ascent (120–134), which served to call God's people to worship in Jerusalem. Psalm 119 depicts the ongoing role of God's law in the life of the faithful. The way forward for God's people in all times involves remembering God's acts of salvation. As we've seen, Israel's faith rested on God's past faithfulness, especially as shown in the exodus from Egypt. Remembering God's works anchors his people in the assurance that true security is found in the Lord alone. Yet the question remains: How do God's people live in light of his grace on a daily basis? What is the roadmap for living in holiness as God's missional people? Psalm 119 responds to these questions in a comprehensive manner.

As a Torah psalm, Psalm 119 instructs God's people how to live faithfully. The Lord shapes us through his law, and the entire structure of the psalm models this. Psalm 119 is an acrostic poem. It uses the twenty-two letters of the Hebrew alphabet in succession to create its message. Its 176 verses break into twenty-two stanzas of eight verses each. In the original Hebrew, the first word of each line begins with the letter of the alphabet used for that stanza: verses 1–8 begin with *aleph*, verses 9–18 begin with *bet*, etc.

There is also a second structure embedded within the acrostic style. This one is thematic and deploys eight terms, one of which appears in virtually every verse. In the NRSV translation, these words are "law," "decrees," "statutes," "commandments," "ordinances," "word," "precepts," and "promise." These terms are broadly synonymous in meaning. They provide a vocabulary for understanding how God reveals his will for his people.

Verses 1–8 serve as the first part of the introduction to the psalm as a whole. It begins with two beatitudes: "Happy are those . . ." (vv. 1–2; cf. Psalm 1:1). "Happy" is the state we abide in when God blesses us. What does such a life look like? It is a life of faithfulness to God's revealed will through the law of the Lord (v. 1), keeping God's decrees (v. 2), and walking in his ways (v. 3). This is not an *earned* happiness through obedience. Rather, it is the outflow of a moment-by-moment relationship in which God communicates (v. 4) and his people respond with a transparent willingness to listen, reflect, and live out what God has spoken through his word.

1. How does Psalm 119 describe the happy life?
2. What role does Scripture play in your growth in God's grace?

FOUR

Psalm 119:9–16

Psalm 119: 9–16 NRSV *How can young people keep their way pure? By guarding it according to your word. [10]With my whole heart I seek you; do not let me stray from your commandments. [11]I treasure your word in my heart, so that I may not sin against you. [12]Blessed are you, O Lord; teach me your statutes. [13]With my lips I declare all the ordinances of your mouth. [14]I delight in the way of your decrees as much as in all riches. [15]I will meditate on your precepts, and fix my eyes on your ways. [16]I will delight in your statutes; I will not forget your word.*

Key Observation. Faithfulness is rooted in a prayerful devotion to God's Word.

Understanding the Word. The Lord shapes us with his Word when we open ourselves fully to its instruction. Psalm 119 is more than simply a call to read Scripture. It is a prayer *of* Scripture, *for* Scripture, and *about* Scripture. As we read portions of Psalm 119 this week (and I encourage you to read through it in its entirety), we find the psalmist not merely providing us with instructions, but also extending praise and petitions to the Lord. Thus, the psalm mixes many of the genres that we've encountered already in the Psalter. Psalm 119 is both a Torah psalm and a prayer for the Lord's help. The Lord's *instruction* is God's answer to our prayers. We'll explore this function by looking at the second half of the introduction to Psalm 119 (vv. 9–16).

First, Psalm 119 is a prayer *of* Scripture. It teaches us to pray for transformation. As a prayer *of* Scripture, this psalm gives us words to voice our desire for faithfulness and our intention to listen earnestly to the Lord. The psalmist reflects on the central role of the Lord's law (*torah*) as instruction. Verse 9 begins with a principle: a person can remain faithful and pure by actively guarding themselves with the help of God's Word. Verses 10–16 are all first-person affirmations of the psalmist's intention to listen attentively and live out God's teaching. These words give voice to the Bible-centered life that the Psalms instruct us to live (cf. Psalms 1 and 19).

But the message of Psalm 119 is not simply a call for us to make a dogged attempt to practice faithfulness out of our own strength. Psalm 119 is also a prayer *for* Scripture. In other words, it is a prayer for God's revelation and for the abundant life that Scripture describes. A consistent prayer throughout Psalm 119 is for the Lord to *instruct* the psalmist. We see this in verse 12: "Teach me your statutes." But such requests are found in almost every stanza (vv. 18, 25–27, 33–39, 64, 66, 73, 124–125, 144, and 169). In the stanzas without a request for instruction, there is typically a petition for God's salvation, blessing, love, or mercy rooted in Scripture (vv. 41, 76–77, 88, 94, 107, 116, 124, 132–134, 146, 149, 153–154, 156, 159, 170, and 175–176). Thus, there is a thread of lament that runs through the psalm. It teaches us how to pray for God's Word and God's salvation as a way of life.

Finally, Psalm 119 is a prayer *about* Scripture. It provides a rich vocabulary by which to reflect on the power of God's Word and to respond in faithfulness, praise, and thanksgiving to the Lord. Verses 9–16 reflect these themes, using language that describes a holistic response with an attitude of openness. Notice the "heart" language in verses 10–11. The psalmist is touched to the core of his being. He responds by treasuring (v. 11) and delighting (vv. 14 and 16) in God's Word (cf. Psalm 1:2). There is also a constant abiding. The psalmist "declares all the ordinances" (v. 13) and "meditates on [God's] precepts" (v. 15). The Word indeed shapes the psalmist's thoughts and actions.

1. How does Psalm 119 serve as a prayer that instructs us?
2. How does Scripture shape your thoughts and actions?

FIVE

Psalm 119:169–176

Psalm 119:169–176 NRSV *Let my cry come before you, O Lord; give me understanding according to your word.* [170]*Let my supplication come before you; deliver me according to your promise.* [171]*My lips will pour forth praise, because you teach me your statutes.* [172]*My tongue will sing of your promise, for all your* *commandments are right. [173]Let your hand be ready to help me, for I have chosen your precepts. [174]I long for your salvation, O Lord, and your law is my delight. [175]Let me live that I may praise you, and let your ordinances help me. [176]I have gone astray like a lost sheep; seek out your servant, for I do not forget your commandments.*

Key Observation. Those who listen attentively to God's Word are transformed into people who praise the Lord in witness to the world.

Understanding the Word. Psalm 119 concludes with a plea for salvation, cleansing, and transformation. Verses 169–176 sound similar to the many laments that we've studied in the Psalter. The difference between Psalm 119 and a true lament psalm is the foundational role played by God's law. As we've seen, virtually every verse includes a reference to the Lord's law (*torah*) or a close synonym.

The psalmist looks to the Lord's instruction as the source for hope. This is an important word for us today. Scripture remains our authoritative guide for what we believe and how we live. It is the map to guide us through the world. In Psalm 118, we saw the ongoing power of the exodus story to shape how God's people understand his ongoing work in the world. Now in Psalm 119, we discover that Scripture is the vehicle by which God continues to speak. The Israelites had access to God's past actions through the witness of the Old Testament scriptures. The "Torah" technically refers to the first five books of the Bible (Genesis–Deuteronomy), but it is likely that the psalmist would have also included Israel's history books and the prophets in referring to the law/*torah*. So the long history of God's faithfulness to Israel becomes part of the *torah*. In addition, today we understand the gospel of Jesus Christ through the teaching of the New Testament books. All of Scripture is our living witness to how God has worked and will continue to work to bring salvation to this world.

As Psalm 119 concludes, the psalmist recognizes his deep need. He cries out to God for understanding (v. 169). He asks God for deliverance based on the hope found in the promises of Scripture (v. 170). He then lifts his voice in praise on account of what God has taught him through the statutes (vv. 171–172, 175). Our testimony of praise serves as the good news for others. Next, he requests God's ever-present help even as he engages with God's precepts (v. 173). The psalmist's delight in God's law increases his longing for the Lord's salvation (v. 174).

The psalmist's prayers reach a climax as he pleads for life so that he might praise the Lord (v. 175). This sums up the goal of the Psalter (see Week 8, Day 5 on Psalms 146–150). In verse 176, the psalmist powerfully confesses his need for cleansing. Thus Psalm 119 ends with confession. The psalmist's engagement with God's Word continually opens him for transformation. It is a transformation for mission.

In Paul's second letter to Timothy, he writes this about Scripture:

> But as for you, continue in what you have learned and firmly believed, knowing from whom you learned it, and how from childhood you have known the sacred writings that are able to instruct you for salvation through faith in Christ Jesus. All scripture is inspired by God and is useful for teaching, for reproof, for correction, and for training in righteousness, so that everyone who belongs to God may be proficient, equipped for every good work. (2 Tim. 3:14–17 NRSV)

Paul's words echo the piety that we've encountered in Psalm 119.

1. What is the connection in Psalm 119 between our need for cleansing, Torah's role in transformation, and our mission in the world?
2. How will you pray differently now based on Psalm 119's teachings?

WEEK FIVE

GATHERING DISCUSSION OUTLINE

A. Open session in prayer. Ask that God would astonish us anew with fresh insight from God's Word and transform us into the disciples that Jesus desires us to become.

B. View the video for this week's readings.

C. What were key insights or takeaways that you gained from your reading during the week and from watching the video commentary? In particular, how did these help you to grow in your faith and understanding of Scripture this week? What parts of the Bible lesson or study raised questions for you?

D. Discuss questions selected from the daily readings.

1. **KEY OBSERVATION:** Thanksgiving is rooted in the loving character of God, who moves to save us in the present just as did in the past.

   DISCUSSION QUESTION: What is the basis for your thanksgiving to the Lord today?

2. **KEY OBSERVATION:** God's victory in the death and resurrection of Jesus is the grounds for celebration and the guarantee of salvation and an abundant future.

   DISCUSSION QUESTION: How does Psalm 118:22–29 enhance our understanding of Jesus' death and resurrection? How does this help us to celebrate God's saving work?

3. **KEY OBSERVATION:** Scripture is God's authoritative instruction to guide the faithful through life.

   DISCUSSION QUESTION: What role does Scripture play in your growth in God's grace?

4. **KEY OBSERVATION:** Faithfulness is rooted in prayerful devotion to God's Word.

   DISCUSSION QUESTION: How does Psalm 119 serve as a prayer that instructs us?

5. **KEY OBSERVATION:** Those who listen attentively to God's Word are transformed into people who praise the Lord in witness to the world.

   DISCUSSION QUESTION: What is the connection in Psalm 119 between our need for cleansing, Torah's role in transformation, and our mission in the world?

E. As the study concludes, consider specific ways that this week's Bible lesson invites you to grow and calls you to change. How do this week's psalms teach us to pray? How do they call us to think differently? How do they challenge us to change in order to align ourselves with God's work in the world? What specific actions should we take to apply the insights of the lesson into our daily lives? What kind of person does our Bible lesson call us to become?

F. Close session with prayer. Emphasize God's ongoing work of transformation in our lives in preparation for loving mission and service in the world. Pray for missing class members as well as for persons whom we need to invite to join our study.

WEEK SIX

Ascending to Worship

Psalms 120–121, 124–125, 130, 133–134

Psalms 120–134 are designated Songs of Ascent and form one of the most memorable blocks of psalms in the Psalter. The precise meaning of this title is debated by scholars, but they are generally believed to be a collection used by pilgrims traveling to God's temple in Jerusalem. As such they were either psalms for the journey or songs sung as worshippers climbed the steps to enter the temple. This week's lessons will focus on Psalms 120–121, 124–125, 130, and 133–134.

The last two weeks we studied psalms associated with the exodus (113, 114, and 118) and the Torah (119). These grounded the renewed life of faith in God's saving actions and the Torah. We will start our study of the Songs of Ascent with Psalm 120, which begins with a pilgrim's prayer.

ONE

Psalm 120

Psalm 120 ESV *In my distress I called to the LORD, and he answered me.*
2Deliver me, O LORD, from lying lips, from a deceitful tongue.
3What shall be given to you, and what more shall be done to you, you deceitful
tongue? 4A warrior's sharp arrows, with glowing coals of the broom tree!
5Woe to me, that I sojourn in Meshech, that I dwell among the tents of Kedar!
6Too long have I had my dwelling among those who hate peace. 7I am for peace,
but when I speak, they are for war!

Key Observation. God's peace does not immunize us from external threats during our journey with him.

Understanding the Word. Pilgrimages require commitment and resilience. They also assume a particular type of person. Psalm 120 describes the core characteristic of a pilgrim in these Songs of Ascent. In verse 7, the psalmist concludes with, "I am for peace." This is the Hebrew term *shalom*, and it is the desired intention of the psalmist. *Shalom* is the goodness, well-being, and abundance found in God. At the beginning of the pilgrimage, the psalmist identifies as one who is *for* God's peace and this will be a recurring theme in the Songs of Ascent (122:6–8; 125:5; and 128:6).

Nonetheless, this psalm is a prayer for protection. Just because one is a person of peace does not make them immune to those who are not. As pilgrims, we long for God's peace. Psalm 120 opens with a declaration of God's faithfulness in answering the pilgrim's previous requests (v. 1). This marks the psalmist as a person of faith. He has experienced God's goodness. This allows him to pray out of deep trust in God's willingness to hear and ability to work salvation.

The psalmist prays about two issues: slanderous attacks (vv. 2–4) and alienation from one's community (vv. 5–7). Both slander and alienation are common experiences. Our faith does not immunize us from them.

In verses 2–4, the psalmist faces the toxic talk of unnamed enemies. The loss of one's reputation is painful. Yet the psalmist recognizes that security does not come from a better public relations campaign or social media strategy, but from the Lord alone. Thus he prays that the Lord's arrows and burning coals will silence the accusers.

Verses 5–7 indicate that the psalmist lived far from Jerusalem. *Meshech* and *Kedar* were places outside of Israel and, for the psalmist, represented the dangers of the wider world. They were full of people who opposed God's peace and desired war. Still, the psalmist declares a commitment to God's peace. May it be so in us as we seek to follow Jesus faithfully in our day.

1. What would it look like if I were truly committed to practicing God's peace (*shalom*) in all aspects of my life?
2. Recall times that you've faced slander or alienation (or some other negative consequence) due to your faith. How does Psalm 120 teach us to pray on such occasions?

TWO

Psalm 121

Psalm 121 *I lift up my eyes to the mountains—where does my help come from?*
[2]My help comes from the LORD, the Maker of heaven and earth.
[3]He will not let your foot slip—he who watches over you will not slumber;
[4]indeed, he who watches over Israel will neither slumber nor sleep.
[5]The LORD watches over you—the LORD is your shade at your right hand;
[6]the sun will not harm you by day, nor the moon by night.
[7]The LORD will keep you from all harm—he will watch over your life; [8]the
LORD will watch over your coming and going both now and forevermore.

Key Observation. As Creator, the Lord serves as eternal guardian over all aspects of our lives.

Understanding the Word. How many of us have ever felt uneasy about a long journey? Before considering a trip, we instinctively ask, "Is it safe to travel there?" Psalm 121 affirms the security that God's people enjoy in him. It unfolds in two parts: the psalmist's question and statement of trust (vv. 1–2) and the community's affirmation of God's ever-present help and security (vv. 3–8).

Verse 1 opens memorably with the psalmist assessing the road ahead. The pilgrim spies a range of mountains and wonders, "Where does my help come from?" These may be the mountains in distant Jerusalem or they may be mountains that the psalmist must climb on the way to worship the Lord. The imagery suggests a couple of options for readers. Mountains were associated with the realms of the gods and were also places of danger for travelers. The psalmist desires security for the journey.

In verse 2, the psalmist answers himself by affirming that the Lord is his help. The Lord is both Helper and the Creator of heaven and earth. This is significant. If one seeks security and help, one must be able to have *full* confidence in the helper. God is not some distant Creator who stands aloof from the affairs of everyday life. He demonstrated power and might in his creation, but Psalm 121 declares the implications of this for everyday life. In particular, the psalm describes God's ability to sustain his people during their journeys.

The perspective shifts between verses 1–2 and 3–8. The psalm moves from first person (I, my) perspective in verses 1–2 to third person statements in verses 3–8. Verses 3–8 contain the words of an outside authority who speaks truth into the psalmist's life, affirming his security in the Lord. Who is this speaker? It could be a priest offering a blessing or a fellow pilgrim. In either case, the intention of verses 3–8 is to provide certainty of God's protection.

Verses 3–8 unfold progressively through three pairs of verses that work together to describe the Lord as the eternal keeper/protector of his people. God is active. Notice the recurring language of the words *watch/keep* (vv. 3–5, 7–8). Verses 3–4 affirm that God's protection can be counted on because the Lord never sleeps. All of us have to sleep at times. But God never does. To say it another way, we can sleep in peace because God always watches over us. Verses 5–6 assert God's protection. Our guardian is our perpetual shade from all harm. Psalm 121 reaches its climax in verses 7–8, which tell us that God's protection is valid for *all life* at *all times* in *all places*. This is good news for us. We may recall Jesus' similar promise: "I am with you always, to the very end of the age" (Matt. 28:20b).

1. How does Psalm 121 describe the Lord? How does this description provide security and assurance?
2. How have you experienced or found security through your faith in the Lord?

THREE

Psalms 124 and 125

Psalms 124 and 125 are celebrations of the security that God's people enjoy in the Lord. Psalm 124 focuses on images of God's work of deliverance in response to the evil that lurks in the world. Psalm 125 centers the security of God's people in Zion—the destination of those on pilgrimage in the Songs of Ascent.

Psalm 124 ESV *If it had not been the LORD who was on our side—let Israel now say—*[2]*if it had not been the LORD who was on our side when people rose up* *against us, [3]then they would have swallowed us up alive, when their anger was kindled against us; [4]then the flood would have swept us away, the torrent would have gone over us; [5]then over us would have gone the raging waters.*

[6]Blessed be the LORD, who has not given us as prey to their teeth! [7]We have escaped like a bird from the snare of the fowlers; the snare is broken, and we have escaped!

[8]Our help is in the name of the LORD, who made heaven and earth.

Psalm 125 ESV *Those who trust in the LORD are like Mount Zion, which cannot be moved, but abides forever. [2]As the mountains surround Jerusalem, so the LORD surrounds his people, from this time forth and forevermore. [3]For the scepter of wickedness shall not rest on the land allotted to the righteous, lest the righteous stretch out their hands to do wrong. [4]Do good, O LORD, to those who are good, and to those who are upright in their hearts! [5]But those who turn aside to their crooked ways the LORD will lead away with evildoers! Peace be upon Israel!*

Key Observation. The Lord is our eternal Helper who frees us to live securely in the present while guaranteeing our future.

Understanding the Word. In Psalm 124, the community testifies to the Lord's faithful work in providing a pathway for God's people to walk securely in the world. This pathway is not always safe, but it is secure. Verse 8 declares the final verdict of Israel's experience: "Our help is in the name of the LORD, who made heaven and earth." This is a rich confession (cf. Psalm 121:2) that summarizes the reality of faith in the Lord. As God's people, we pray "in the name of the LORD" on the assumption that God does indeed hear and answer us. Verse 8 affirms this truth.

Verses 1–5 confess that Israel exists solely due to God's gracious acts of deliverance. This is an acknowledgment of radical dependence. The threats and dangers of the life of faith are real. This psalm reminds us of God's protection from enemies (vv. 2b–3) and overwhelming threats during our journey (vv. 4–5). Verses 6–7 liken our deliverance in the Lord to a bird that has been freed from the hunter's trap. Security and help belong to the Lord who is on the side of his people. This does not mean that God is *against* all others. In fact, the Lord works on behalf of his people ultimately for the benefit of all other nations. Indeed, it will be through Israel that the Lord will bless all creation, extending that blessing through the life, death, and resurrection of Jesus. God's people serve as agents and witnesses of this desire to bless.

Psalm 125 anchors the security of God's people in Mount Zion. Zion refers to the hill in Jerusalem where the temple stood. It represented the earthly seat of the Lord's power (Psalm 48). Within the Songs of Ascent, Zion is the end of the journey and serves as an anchor in the stormy sea of chaos that God's people faced along the way. This psalm reminds God's people that the Lord's reign has a moral and ethical dimension. The Lord is for righteousness/uprightness (vv. 3–4) and peace (v. 5). It is a prayer for God's goodness to manifest itself in the lives of the faithful.

As followers of Jesus, Zion/Jerusalem is now replaced as the focal point of faith by the life, death, and resurrection of Jesus and the indwelling work of the Spirit in our lives. Our pilgrimage is not to a place but to people who need to hear the gospel from us. We journey in the confidence that Jesus leads us into the world on mission (Matthew 28:18–20) in the power of the Spirit (Acts 1:8).

1. What are some of the greatest challenges you have faced as a follower of Jesus? How have you experienced the Lord as your help?
2. What does it mean for the world that God is for his people?

FOUR

Psalm 130

Psalm 130 NRSV *Out of the depths I cry to you, O Lord.* [2]*Lord, hear my voice!*
Let your ears be attentive to the voice of my supplications!

[3]*If you, O Lord, should mark iniquities, Lord, who could stand?* [4]*But there is*
forgiveness with you, so that you may be revered.

[5]*I wait for the Lord, my soul waits, and in his word I hope;* [6]*my soul waits*
for the Lord more than those who watch for the morning, more than those who watch for the morning.

[7]*O Israel, hope in the Lord! For with the Lord there is steadfast love, and with him is great power to redeem.* [8]*It is he who will redeem Israel from all its*
iniquities.

Key Observation. When we are overwhelmed by life's circumstances, we can find hope in the Lord's steadfast love and forgiveness.

Understanding the Word. Psalm 130 is the sixth of the seven psalms recognized as guides for praying for forgiveness (cf. 6, 32, 38, 51, 102, and 143). This psalm serves as a model prayer combining a poignant cry for forgiveness with deep trust and an intention to testify to the wider community about the Lord's goodness. The psalm has played a significant role in the life of key leaders in the church. The sixteenth-century reformer Martin Luther believed this psalm summarized the gospel. On May 24, 1738, the day when John Wesley experienced his "heart strangely warmed," he also listened to a choir sing this psalm at St. Paul's cathedral.

Psalm 130 is memorable for its desperate opening appeal to the Lord (vv. 1–2). "Depths" is shorthand for the "depths of the sea" (Isaiah 51:10; Ezekiel 27:34). The psalmist feels as though he is drowning. How many times have we experienced life in a state of being overwhelmed and fearful? Psalm 130 testifies to a hopeful ending in such times. The bleakness of the psalmist's outlook in the moment does not blind him to an alternative possibility. In fact, the psalmist hedges all of his bets on a truth that he holds tightly within his being.

Verses 1–2 remind us that we can always turn to the Lord in prayer regardless of how extreme or hopeless our situation may appear. Verses 3–4 speak of the profound mercy of God. The Lord is a God who forgives. This is at the heart of the gospel. John reminds us, "If we say that we have no sin, we deceive ourselves, and the truth is not in us. If we confess our sins, he who is faithful and just will forgive us our sins and cleanse us from all unrighteousness" (1 John 1:8–9 NRSV).

What does this mean for the psalmist and for us? We can pray to God in our most desperate times with the assurance that our sins do not prevent him from helping us. The Lord is not some great bookkeeper in the heavens who watches us only to record our sins. Instead, the psalmist affirms that he is a God who forgives. We can thus fear and revere the Lord because of his mercy rather than out of a fear of punishment.

How do we live in times of desperate circumstances? In the second half of the psalm (vv. 5–8), the psalmist shows the way. In verses 5–6, the psalmist affirms a deep longing for the Lord. He waits in eager anticipation of deliverance in the same way that a night guardsman watches for the dawn. Psalm 130 concludes by testifying to the entire community of faith (vv. 7–8): put your hope in the Lord. In God alone, you will find steadfast love, redemption, and forgiveness. This is good news. You can bank on it even in your most desperate hours.

1. What does Psalm 130 teach us about praying for forgiveness?
2. What is the basis of the psalmist's hope? How would such a perspective impact your life?

FIVE

Psalms 133 and 134

The Songs of Ascent conclude with two brief psalms (133 and 134). Psalm 133 is a celebration of the unified community of faith. Psalm 134 is a song of blessing and serves as a fitting conclusion to this collection.

Psalm 133 ESV *Behold, how good and pleasant it is when brothers dwell in unity!* 2*It is like the precious oil on the head, running down on the beard, on the beard of Aaron, running down on the collar of his robes!* 3*It is like the dew of Hermon, which falls on the mountains of Zion! For there the LORD has commanded the blessing, life forevermore.*

Psalm 134 ESV *Come, bless the LORD, all you servants of the LORD, who stand by night in the house of the LORD!* 2*Lift up your hands to the holy place and bless the LORD!*

3*May the LORD bless you from Zion, he who made heaven and earth!*

Key Observation. A community that lives in unity and praises the Lord is a potent witness and testimony to the world.

Understanding the Word. The Songs of Ascent celebrate the pilgrimage of the faithful to Jerusalem. Psalm 133 makes explicit the importance of the community as a whole in this journey. The Christian life is not a solo act. In the life of faith, we may find profound frustration and even hostility between brothers and sisters in Christ. This is a sad reality, but Psalm 133 reminds us that disunity and tension do not have to have the final word.

God's people share a common bond that transcends all perceived differences. Those who gathered in Jerusalem came from different families and regions, but they found unity in their commitment to the Lord. This psalm uses two images to portray the abundance that God's people enjoy as one body. First, in verse 2, the psalmist imagines an outpouring of oil flowing down the beard of Aaron onto his robes at his ordination. All that was required was an anointing of oil, but here we find a flood. Second, in verse 3, unity is likened to the dew of Mount Hermon. Hermon was a mountain approximately 125 miles north of Jerusalem. It was known as a source of abundant moisture in an otherwise dry region. Both of these symbols in Psalm 133 function to emphasize the true potential of community. The community of God's people is a gift of exuberant abundance. The walls that divide us have been broken down. As Paul says, "There is neither Jew nor Greek, there is neither slave nor free, there is no male and female, for you are all one in Christ Jesus" (Gal. 3:28 ESV). In Christian tradition, this psalm is often read during celebrations of the Lord's Supper, in which we remember that the body of Jesus was broken so that we might be made whole.

Psalm 134 calls the community to praise and worship the Lord in anticipation of his blessing. It is a final evening service before the pilgrims return home. "Bless" occurs in all three verses of this short psalm. As we saw in Psalm 103, humans *bless* the Lord through acts of praise. Verses 1–2 call on God's people who have gathered for worship in Jerusalem to lift up their hands and praise the Lord in a final act of worship.

This psalm ends with a reciprocal blessing from the Lord to the people (v. 3). This blessing is not a *quid pro quo*. The Lord is the Maker of heaven and earth (Psalm 121:2). Yet he freely chooses to bless his people as a witness to his relationship with them. This is a sign to the world that blessing is found in the Lord.

1. What are your experiences of Christian community? Who are the brothers and sisters in Christ who support you in your walk with God?
2. How does the worship of the Lord and God's blessings on his people serve as a witness to the world?

WEEK SIX

GATHERING DISCUSSION OUTLINE

A. Open session in prayer. Ask that God would astonish us anew with fresh insight from God's Word and transform us into the disciples that Jesus desires us to become.

B. View video for this week's readings.

C. What were key insights or takeaways that you gained from your reading during the week and from watching the video commentary? In particular, how did these help you to grow in your faith and understanding of Scripture this week? What parts of the Bible lesson or study raised questions for you?

D. Discuss questions selected from the daily readings.

1. **KEY OBSERVATION:** God's peace does not immunize us from external threats during our journey with him.

   DISCUSSION QUESTION: Recall times that you've faced slander or alienation (or some other negative consequence) due to your faith. How does Psalm 120 teach us to pray on such occasions?

2. **KEY OBSERVATION:** As Creator, the Lord serves as eternal guardian over all aspects of our lives.

   DISCUSSION QUESTION: How does Psalm 121 describe the Lord? How does this description provide security and assurance?

3. **KEY OBSERVATION:** The Lord is our eternal Helper who frees us to live securely in the present while guaranteeing our future.

   DISCUSSION QUESTION: What are some of the greatest challenges you have faced as a follower of Jesus? How have you experienced the Lord as your help?

4. **KEY OBSERVATION:** When we are overwhelmed by life's circumstances, we can find hope in the Lord's steadfast love and forgiveness.

   DISCUSSION QUESTION: What does Psalm 130 teach us about praying for forgiveness?

5. **KEY OBSERVATION:** A community that lives in unity and praises the Lord is a potent witness and testimony to the world.

   DISCUSSION QUESTION: What are your experiences of Christian community? Who are the brothers and sisters in Christ who support you in your walk with God?

E. As the study concludes, consider specific ways that this week's Bible lesson invites you to grow and calls you to change. How do this week's psalms teach us to pray? How do they call us to think differently? How do they challenge us to change in order to align ourselves with God's work in the world? What specific actions should we take to apply the insights of the lesson into our daily lives? What kind of person does our Bible lesson call us to become?

F. Close session with prayer. Emphasize God's ongoing work of transformation in our lives in preparation for loving mission and service in the world. Pray for missing class members as well as for persons whom we need to invite to join our study.

WEEK SEVEN

Making Sense of Our Past

Psalms 135, 136, 137, 139

History is a funny thing. It is a testimony about the past that attempts to make sense of our present. Yet history can take on different shapes and meanings. We've already looked at the historical psalms which concluded Book IV of the Psalter (105–106). These used Israel's past as a means of giving thanks for God's faithfulness (Psalm 105), but also to recount Israel's many sins (Psalm 106) as a means of asking for deliverance.

This week we will look at three psalms (135, 136, 137) that look explicitly at Israel's past. Psalm 135 calls God's people to praise the Lord for who he is and what he has done. Psalm 136 will describe God's glorious acts on behalf of his people. Psalm 137 explores the horror of exile and the intense faith that sustained the community. We will then conclude with a Davidic psalm (139) that explores his personal past, as well as how to pray when surrounded by enemies. These psalms together will help us make sense of the totality of our history: the good, the bad, and the personal.

ONE

Psalm 135

Psalm 135 ESV *Praise the Lord! Praise the name of the Lord, give praise,*
O servants of the Lord, 2who stand in the house of the Lord, in the courts of
the house of our God! 3Praise the Lord, for the Lord is good; sing to his name,
for it is pleasant! 4For the Lord has chosen Jacob for himself, Israel as his own
possession.

5For I know that the Lord is great, and that our Lord is above all gods.
6Whatever the Lord pleases, he does, in heaven and on earth, in the seas and

all deeps. 7He it is who makes the clouds rise at the end of the earth, who makes
lightnings for the rain and brings forth the wind from his storehouses.
8He it was who struck down the firstborn of Egypt, both of man and of beast;
9who in your midst, O Egypt, sent signs and wonders against Pharaoh and all his
servants; 10who struck down many nations and killed mighty kings, 11Sihon, king
of the Amorites, and Og, king of Bashan, and all the kingdoms of Canaan, 12and
gave their land as a heritage, a heritage to his people Israel.
13Your name, O LORD, endures forever, your renown, O LORD, throughout
all ages. 14For the LORD will vindicate his people and have compassion on his
servants.
15The idols of the nations are silver and gold, the work of human hands.
16They have mouths, but do not speak; they have eyes, but do not see; 17they have
ears, but do not hear, nor is there any breath in their mouths. 18Those who make
them become like them, so do all who trust in them.
19O house of Israel, bless the LORD! O house of Aaron, bless the LORD! 20O
house of Levi, bless the LORD! You who fear the LORD, bless the LORD! 21Blessed
be the LORD from Zion, he who dwells in Jerusalem! Praise the LORD!

Key Observation. The Lord's gracious actions on behalf of his people are a witness and invitation to the world.

Understanding the Word. Psalm 135 reminds us of a foundational truth. There may be other beings called "gods," but they pale in comparison to the one true God, the Lord. The Israelites were surrounded by nations who neither knew nor worshipped the Lord. These nations exalted scores of gods and goddesses. As we know from Israel's history, many of these people—such as the Egyptians, the Philistines, the Assyrians, and the Babylonians—often threatened and oppressed God's people. Yet, Scripture makes a profound counterclaim. There is only one true God and he makes himself known first through his people, Israel, and then ultimately through Jesus Christ.

Psalm 135 begins (vv. 1–4) and ends (vv. 19–21) by calling Israel to praise the Lord. Verse 4 reminds us that God has called a people to himself. Israel was God's "own possession" (Exodus 19:5; Deuteronomy 7:6, 14:2). The phrase "own possession" can also be translated "treasured possession." God's people hold a special place in his heart and mission (Genesis 12:3; Exodus 19:4–6).

They are to be agents of blessing to all nations. God is not *for* Israel and *against* all other nations; rather God is *for* Israel *for the sake of all peoples*.

The basis for praise in this psalm is God's position in contrast to other gods (v. 4). The Lord is categorically different. First, he is the Creator of all (vv. 5–7). Second, verses 8–15 recite God's mighty acts of salvation in the exodus from Egypt and the gift of the land of Canaan. What other god has done such a thing for a people?

Indeed, the worship of lifeless idols is not just ironic, it's silly (vv. 15–18). Idols represent mere human power and ideas. They are mute, blind, deaf—in other words, powerless. The Lord revealed his true power through the coming of Jesus, who took on real flesh and blood. He could be heard, touched, and spoken with. The risen Jesus abides with us still as we testify to the world that God truly loves us and acts for our good.

1. What is the basis for biblical claims about the incomparability of the Lord?
2. How does your life witness to God's graciousness in ways that are evident to others?

TWO

Psalm 136

Psalm 136 is a celebration of God's faithful love. It serves as a guide for giving a testimony of gratitude for how God has sustained his people and always been available when we are in need. It unfolds as a call and response that alternates between the Lord's gracious acts and the people's recurring response of gratitude rooted in God's loving commitment to them. Given its length, we will only explore select verses.

Psalm 136 NRSV *O give thanks to the Lord, for he is good, for his steadfast love*
endures forever. [2]O give thanks to the God of gods, for his steadfast love endures
forever. [3]O give thanks to the Lord of lords, for his steadfast love endures forever;
[4]who alone does great wonders, for his steadfast love endures forever; [5]who
by understanding made the heavens, for his steadfast love endures forever; [6]who

spread out the earth on the waters, for his steadfast love endures forever; [7]who made the great lights, for his steadfast love endures forever; [8]the sun to rule over the day, for his steadfast love endures forever; [9]the moon and stars to rule over the night, for his steadfast love endures forever;

[10]who struck Egypt through their firstborn, for his steadfast love endures forever; [11]and brought Israel out from among them, for his steadfast love endures forever; [12]with a strong hand and an outstretched arm, for his steadfast love endures forever; [13]who divided the Red Sea in two, for his steadfast love endures forever; [14]and made Israel pass through the midst of it, for his steadfast love endures forever; [15]but overthrew Pharaoh and his army in the Red Sea, for his steadfast love endures forever; [16]who led his people through the wilderness, for his steadfast love endures forever; [17]who struck down great kings, for his steadfast love endures forever; [18]and killed famous kings, for his steadfast love endures forever; [19]Sihon, king of the Amorites, for his steadfast love endures forever; [20]and Og, king of Bashan, for his steadfast love endures forever; [21]and gave their land as a heritage, for his steadfast love endures forever; [22]a heritage to his servant Israel, for his steadfast love endures forever.

[23]It is he who remembered us in our low estate, for his steadfast love endures forever; [24]and rescued us from our foes, for his steadfast love endures forever; [25]who gives food to all flesh, for his steadfast love endures forever.

[26]O give thanks to the God of heaven, for his steadfast love endures forever.

Key Observation. Worship the Lord for his faithful and steadfast love that creates, saves, and sustains.

Understanding the Word. Psalm 136 is audacious in its certainty about the goodness of God. This certainty is not solely based on personal experience, but is rooted in the entire community's history. Our present reality is insufficient for making sense of life, especially when we find ourselves in times of loss and uncertainty. Psalm 136 acknowledges such difficult times. Read between the lines of verses 23–25. These verses affirm God's faithfulness and salvation, but they also show personal acquaintance with human pain—times of humiliation and oppression (v. 23), days when enemies came close to achieving victory (v. 24), and seasons of hunger and lack (v. 25). Yet Psalm 136 proclaims this truth: the Lord's loyal love is forever. It is inexhaustible. It shows up during good times and bad. We can trust in God because he has demonstrated over the long haul that he does indeed have our best interests at heart.

Psalm 136 frames its historical testimony with a call to thanksgiving (vv. 1–3 and 26). The psalmist reviews history in order to provide a recipe for thanksgiving that includes God's mighty acts in creating the world (vv. 4–9) and saving Israel (vv. 10–22). He concludes with open-ended language that empowers God's people to give thanks for the present (vv. 23–25).

Verses 1–3 address the Lord as Yahweh (God's personal name). Yahweh is "God of gods" and "Lord of lords" (vv. 2–3). This is a reminder of the Lord's incomparability with any other being. God's steadfast love (*hesed*) is the foundation. *Hesed* is a central component of God's character. When we say, "God is love," we are not making a mere sentimental statement but declaring that *hesed* is at the core of God's essence. It is God's active, loyal, faithful love. It is the love that keeps, restores, and delivers.

God demonstrates *hesed* in human history. It is not mythic or something merely hoped for. It is real and God's "great wonders" (v. 4) demonstrate it's reality. There is no other being with this track record. Verses 5–22 recount the story of creation and God's gracious actions for Israel in the exodus, wilderness, and inheritance of the land of Canaan. When we read Psalm 136, we inherit this history. Verses 23–25 shift to the present and we encounter "us" language. The God who saved is the God who saves.

Psalm 136 is not the final word on God's actions. The New Testament witnesses to the climax of God's work of salvation through the life, death, and resurrection of Jesus Christ, the Son of God and our Savior. As Paul wrote, "But God proves his love for us in that while we still were sinners Christ died for us" (Rom. 5:8 NRSV). We are living witnesses of this truth and we await eagerly the new creation (Revelation 21:1–6) when God will make all things new.

1. How does remembering God's past faithfulness help you to give thanks and pray today?
2. Why is it important to have a long view of history and God's role in it? How does this give you hope for your future?

THREE
Psalm 137:1–6

Psalm 137 is one of the richest in terms of the commitment to faith expressed (vv. 1–6). It is also most startling in its honest longing for vindication from the horrors experienced at the hands of others (vv. 7–19). We will spend two days on this short psalm in order to make sense of its potential to deepen our faith and help us to pray in our darkest moments (or when we meet someone who has been victimized cruelly by the powerful). Today we will cover the initial six verses of Psalm 137.

Psalm 137:1–6 *By the rivers of Babylon we sat and wept when we remembered Zion.* [2]*There on the poplars we hung our harps,* [3]*for there our captors asked us for songs, our tormentors demanded songs of joy; they said, "Sing us one of the songs of Zion!"*

[4]*How can we sing the songs of the LORD while in a foreign land?* [5]*If I forget you, Jerusalem, may my right hand forget its skill.* [6]*May my tongue cling to the roof of my mouth if I do not remember you, if I do not consider Jerusalem my highest joy.*

Key Observation. Sacred memory serves as a light to sustain us even in the darkest moments of our lives.

Understanding the Word. Psalm 137 teaches us that there is no experience out of bounds for our prayer life. As we've read Israel's historical psalms, we've encountered despair and defeat, but Israel's darkest hour included the destruction of Jerusalem (including the temple), the loss of the Davidic kingship, and the exile to Babylon. These realities serve as the backdrop for Psalm 137.

The psalm opens memorably with a portrait of life in exile (vv. 1–3). The psalmist recalls times when God's people sat and wept thinking about their losses. Their sense of loss centered on Zion. The city and its temple were now *past* history. This memory was painful. The biting cruelty of their captors only heightened the pain. It was not enough to simply destroy the institutions that gave meaning to their lives. It was not enough to drag them hundreds of miles from their homeland. On top of this, the Babylonians added mocking requests for God's people to sing their religious songs about Zion and the greatness of their God (e.g., Psalms 46 or 48). These opening verses show the depths to which the Babylonians went to heap further humiliations upon Israel. These are blatant and excessive acts of evil by the powerful over the powerless. The forlorn among God's people cry out, "How can we sing the songs of the LORD while in a foreign land?" (v. 4).

Yet God's people find a counter testimony to proclaim a different reality. It is at the very pit of their pain that this psalm takes a dramatic turn. Instead of deeper despair, Israel finds hope because the memory of Zion is real and God cannot be erased by destroying buildings made by human hands or even by afflicting his people with violence and humiliating indignities. In verses 5–6, the psalmist pivots to a renewed faith and a poignant prayer of resistance in the face of the pain of exile. For the Israelites, Jerusalem/Zion served as the locus for their trust in the Lord. By answering the abuse of the Babylonians with vocal memory of Zion, God's people found renewed strength. Verses 5–6 serve as an oath to never forget Jerusalem and keep it as their highest joy.

Psalm 137 invites us to reflect on the deepest tragedies of our lives while affirming that we cling steadfastly to the living embodiment of Jerusalem/Zion, the Word made flesh in Jesus Christ (John 1:14) who suffered yet triumphed in resurrection.

1. What have been some of your darkest moments in life? What challenges did they present to your understanding of faith?
2. How does sacred memory help the psalmist in the midst of the chaos of exile?

FOUR

Psalm 137:7–9

Psalm 137:7–9 *Remember, LORD, what the Edomites did on the day Jerusalem fell. "Tear it down," they cried, "tear it down to its foundations!" [8]Daughter Babylon, doomed to destruction, happy is the one who repays you according to what you have done to us. [9]Happy is the one who seizes your infants and dashes them against the rocks.*

Key Observation. Despite our pain, we can bring our darkest thoughts to light in prayer by relinquishing them to a loving and just God.

Understanding the Word. Psalm 137:7–9 contains words that we should hope we never have to pray. The first six verses of the psalm offered a poignant portrait of restored faith and hope during the darkest days. The final three verses articulate this renewed hope in prayer against the perpetrators of violence. This prayer is a cry for vengeance against those who victimized God's people during the destruction of Jerusalem and subsequent exile. Verse 7 recalls the role that Edom played in siding with the Babylonians (Obadiah 11–14). But the strongest words are reserved for the Babylonians. Verses 8–9 twice use the word "happy" (NRSV), which occurs twenty-six times in the Psalms (e.g., Psalms 1:1; 2:12; 32:1). This is the only usage in which the context is a prayer *against* others. The imagery of verse 9 is terrifying: "Happy is the one who seizes your infants and dashes them against the rocks." Presumably this is a prayer for reciprocal action against the Babylonians for the atrocities experienced by God's people during and after the siege of Jerusalem. In other words, God's people had witnessed the Babylonians killing their children in this manner.

What role does such a prayer for vengeance serve in the life of Christ's followers today? Didn't Jesus teach his disciples to move away from an "eye for an eye mentality" by turning the other cheek and to love their enemies (Matthew 5:38–39, 43–44)? And didn't Paul call God's people to overcome evil with good (Romans 12:19–21) by reminding us of another Old Testament teaching: "It is mine to avenge; I will repay" (Deut. 32:35)?

I began the commentary by saying that verses 7–9 are words that we should hope we never have to pray. However, they offer us a critical message that there is a place for such language when we have found ourselves victimized. These prayers for vengeance are not words of the powerful poised to unleash wrath on an enemy. These are the words of vanquished and abused victims of violent and dehumanizing actions who feel true rage but have no way of expressing it or acting on it. This is the crucial point. Psalm 137 is about the restoration of faith for the victims of exile. The words of verses 7–9 are a prayer of *surrender* and *submission*, not to the evil powers of oppression and violence, but to the Lord. These words release the deepest pain and rage to God and leave judgment in God's hands alone. Rather than suppressing our darkest thoughts,

Psalm 137 points to healing through speaking our feelings to God. When we can openly survey our deepest pain and release it, along with any desire for retribution and justice to God, then we can make sense of the past and begin to live again in the hope of full restoration.

1. How does Psalm 137:7–9 challenge the way that you understand prayer?
2. How does Psalm 137:7–9 help us to make sense of our deepest pain?

FIVE

Psalm 139

Psalm 139 ESV *O Lord, you have searched me and known me!* [2]*You know*
when I sit down and when I rise up; you discern my thoughts from afar. [3]*You*
search out my path and my lying down and are acquainted with all my ways.
[4]*Even before a word is on my tongue, behold, O Lord, you know it altogether.*
[5]*You hem me in, behind and before, and lay your hand upon me.* [6]*Such knowl-*
edge is too wonderful for me; it is high; I cannot attain it.

[7]*Where shall I go from your Spirit? Or where shall I flee from your presence?*
[8]*If I ascend to heaven, you are there! If I make my bed in Sheol, you are there!*
[9]*If I take the wings of the morning and dwell in the uttermost parts of the sea,*
[10]*even there your hand shall lead me, and your right hand shall hold me.* [11]*If I*
say, "Surely the darkness shall cover me, and the light about me be night," [12]*even*
the darkness is not dark to you; the night is bright as the day, for darkness is as
light with you.

[13]*For you formed my inward parts; you knitted me together in my mother's*
womb. [14]*I praise you, for I am fearfully and wonderfully made. Wonderful are*
your works; my soul knows it very well. [15]*My frame was not hidden from you,*
when I was being made in secret, intricately woven in the depths of the earth.
[16]*Your eyes saw my unformed substance; in your book were written, every one*
of them, the days that were formed for me, when as yet there was none of them.

[17]*How precious to me are your thoughts, O God! How vast is the sum of*
them! [18]*If I would count them, they are more than the sand. I awake, and I am*
still with you.

[19]Oh that you would slay the wicked, O God! O men of blood, depart from me! [20]They speak against you with malicious intent; your enemies take your name in vain. [21]Do I not hate those who hate you, O LORD? And do I not loathe those who rise up against you? [22]I hate them with complete hatred; I count them my enemies.

[23]Search me, O God, and know my heart! Try me and know my thoughts!
[24]And see if there be any grievous way in me, and lead me in the way everlasting!

Key Observation. God knows us at the core of our being and we need to be open to his ongoing work of transformation.

Understanding the Word. Psalm 139 captures the intimacy of a moment-by-moment relationship with God. It is part of the final group of Davidic psalms in the Psalter (138–145). Psalm 139 is one of the most personal of the psalms. The psalmist's core desire is profound formation in the "way everlasting" (v. 24). This psalm also offers a challenging section (vv. 19–22) where the psalmist prays explicitly against the wicked by asking God to kill them (v. 19). The reconciliation of these two sections will conclude our reflection today. Psalm 139 fits our theme of "Making Sense of Our Past" through its reflection on life with God in a world that often stands *against* the values of his kingdom.

The psalm unfolds through four equal sections of six verses. Thematically these four sections break into two larger units: verses 1–18 and 19–24. The language of "searching and knowing" (vv. 1 and 23–24) frames the psalm. The focus is on the relationship between the psalmist and God. We've encountered plenty of psalms that use first-person language in addressing God, but most other psalms with an individual focus turn at some point to include Israel as a whole (e.g., Psalms 3; 121; 130).

Verse 1 affirms that the Lord knows everything about the psalmist. There is no indication of any limits on what God knows about the psalmist. The word "know" recurs throughout the psalm (vv. 1, 2, 4, 6, 14, and 23). The psalmist is an open book before God and this is a comfort to him. God *knows* us. We do not need to wear masks or put up fronts with God.

In verses 1–6, God is the subject of all of the actions. The psalmist has experienced God as the One who knows and guides all of life. Verses 7–12 shift to give the psalmist's perspective on the relationship. He testifies to God's all-encompassing presence. There is no place or situation where God is absent. Verses 13–18 merge the first two sections together through the psalmist's reflection on and praise for God's care for him. This care began in his mother's womb and extends to all that will occur during his life. This is an affirmation of security. God holds our lives in his hands.

Verses 19–24 shift the tone in a surprising way. The psalmist calls for God's elimination of the wicked and those who hate the Lord. *Hate* is not an attitude but an action. To hate the wicked means to stand in opposition to them. The psalmist recognizes that the presence of evil and sin is a blemish on creation. Perhaps the wicked were actively persecuting the psalmist and his community (Psalm 137). Verses 19–22 are a radical way for the psalmist to proclaim his loyalty to the God who has "searched and known" him (v. 1). In fact, the psalm ends with a request for a deeper cleansing from God. To proclaim one's loyalty and set oneself apart from the wicked *assumes* that one is walking with integrity and clean hands. Verses 23–24 serve as a model prayer for us as we seek to represent the way of Jesus today.

1. What does Psalm 139 teach us about the meaning of our relationship with God?
2. What kind of person do we need to become in order to pray this psalm with integrity? Is there any part of you that needs a deeper cleansing by the Lord (vv. 23–24)?

WEEK SEVEN

GATHERING DISCUSSION OUTLINE

A. Open session in prayer. Ask that God would astonish us anew with fresh insight from God's Word and transform us into the disciples that Jesus desires us to become.

B. View video for this week's readings.

C. What were key insights or takeaways that you gained from your reading during the week and from watching the video commentary? In particular, how did these help you to grow in your faith and understanding of Scripture this week? What parts of the Bible lesson or study raised questions for you?

D. Discuss questions selected from the daily readings.

1. **KEY OBSERVATION:** The Lord's gracious actions on behalf of his people are a witness and invitation to the world.

   DISCUSSION QUESTION: What is the basis for biblical claims about the incomparability of the Lord?

2. **KEY OBSERVATION:** Worship the Lord for his faithful and steadfast love that creates, saves, and sustains.

   DISCUSSION QUESTION: How does remembering God's past faithfulness help you to give thanks and pray today?

3. **KEY OBSERVATION:** Sacred memory serves as a light to sustain us even in the darkest moments of our lives.

DISCUSSION QUESTION: How does sacred memory help the psalmist in the midst of the chaos of exile?

4. **KEY OBSERVATION:** Despite our pain, we can bring our darkest thoughts to light in prayer by relinquishing them to a loving and just God.

   DISCUSSION QUESTION: How does Psalm 137:7–9 challenge the way that you understand prayer?

5. **KEY OBSERVATION:** God knows us at the core of our being and we need to be open to his ongoing work of transformation.

   DISCUSSION QUESTION: What kind of person do we need to become in order to pray this psalm with integrity? Is there any part of you that needs a deeper cleansing by the Lord (vv. 23–24)?

E. As the study concludes, consider specific ways that this week's Bible lesson invites you to grow and calls you to change. How do this week's psalms teach us to pray? How do they call us to think differently? How do they challenge us to change in order to align ourselves with God's work in the world? What specific actions should we take to apply the insights of the lesson into our daily lives? What kind of person does our Bible lesson call us to become?

F. Close session with prayer. Emphasize God's ongoing work of transformation in our lives in preparation for loving mission and service in the world. Pray for missing class members as well as for persons whom we need to invite to join our study.

WEEK EIGHT

David's Final Word: Prayer and Praise as a Way of Life

Psalms 138, 140, 144–150

The focus in our final week of study is twofold. On Days 1–4, we will read four Davidic psalms (138, 140, 144, and 145). On Day 5, we will conclude our study of the Psalter by summarizing the journey through this rich book through the lens of worship in Psalms 146–150. It is fitting that the Psalter returns to a block of Davidic psalms before its concluding chorus of praise. Psalms labeled, "Of David," make up about half of the 150 psalms, but most of them appear in Books I–III (Psalms 1–89). In fact, Psalms 138–145 is the largest group of psalms in Books IV and V (Psalms 90–150) attributed to David. The only other Davidic psalms in these last two books are Psalms 101, 103, and 108–110. This suggests that grouping these eight Davidic psalms immediately before the final, climactic Hallelujah (Praise the Lord) psalms was intentional.

ONE

Psalm 138

Psalm 138 ESV *I give you thanks, O Lord, with my whole heart; before the gods I sing your praise; [2]I bow down toward your holy temple and give thanks to your name for your steadfast love and your faithfulness, for you have exalted above all things your name and your word. [3]On the day I called, you answered me; my strength of soul you increased.*

[4]All the kings of the earth shall give you thanks, O Lord, for they have heard the words of your mouth, [5]and they shall sing of the ways of the Lord, for great is the glory of the Lord. [6]For though the Lord is high, he regards the lowly, but the haughty he knows from afar.

[7]Though I walk in the midst of trouble, you preserve my life; you stretch out your hand against the wrath of my enemies, and your right hand delivers me.
[8]The LORD will fulfill his purpose for me; your steadfast love, O LORD, endures forever. Do not forsake the work of your hands.

Key Observation. God's steadfast love is the reason for giving thanks to him and testifying of his faithfulness before the nations.

Understanding the Word. Profoundly, Psalm 138's prayer of thanksgiving follows the intense rage of Psalm 137. In the latter, God's people languished in exile (137:1–4). In order to publicly humiliate them, the Babylonians asked them to sing songs about Zion. The psalm ended with a prayer of retribution against the oppressors. This release of rage opened up a future for the victims of oppression.

Now in Psalm 138, David leads a chorus of thanksgiving in the midst of the nations. Verse 1 is the fitting response to the question posed in 137:4, "How can we sing the songs of the LORD while in a foreign land?" David sings God's praises before the gods. God's people serve as witnesses to the true King by practicing faithfulness because of the steadfast love and faithfulness of the Lord (138:2). Despite the chaos and pain of the exile, the Lord remains exalted (v. 2) and answers prayer (v. 3).

In verses 4–6, David envisions the nations acknowledging the Lord and giving thanks to him. They recognize his greatness (v. 5). Yet this is no power play. In verse 6, the Lord specifically aligns with the lowly (cf. Psalm 113:4–9). "Lowly" here refers to God's people (cf. Psalms 136:23–26 and 137). The Lord manifests his great love and faithfulness by redeeming his people from oppression and evil. Most profoundly this included bringing the Babylonian exile to an end by returning his people back to the land (Ezra 1–3).

Psalm 138 ends with a hopeful statement of trust (vv. 6–8). David recognizes the troubles and sufferings of life, yet he testifies to the Lord's ongoing protection. He also witnesses to the good purposes that God has for him rooted in God's eternal, faithful love. This is good news as we journey through the world on mission. It's a promise that will sustain us.

1. How does Psalm 138 teach us to give thanks when we find ourselves in the midst of a world that doesn't yet know Jesus as Lord?

2. How does Psalm 138 explain the significance of God's steadfast love and its role in the psalmist's life?

TWO

Psalm 140

Psalm 140 *Rescue me, LORD, from evildoers; protect me from the violent, [2]who devise evil plans in their hearts and stir up war every day. [3]They make their tongues as sharp as a serpent's; the poison of vipers is on their lips.*

[4]Keep me safe, LORD, from the hands of the wicked; protect me from the violent, who devise ways to trip my feet. [5]The arrogant have hidden a snare for me; they have spread out the cords of their net and have set traps for me along my path.

[6]I say to the LORD, "You are my God." Hear, LORD, my cry for mercy. [7]Sovereign LORD, my strong deliverer, you shield my head in the day of battle. [8]Do not grant the wicked their desires, LORD; do not let their plans succeed.

[9]Those who surround me proudly rear their heads; may the mischief of their lips engulf them. [10]May burning coals fall on them; may they be thrown into the fire, into miry pits, never to rise. [11]May slanderers not be established in the land; may disaster hunt down the violent.

[12]I know that the LORD secures justice for the poor and upholds the cause of the needy. [13]Surely the righteous will praise your name, and the upright will live in your presence.

Key Observation. The Lord invites us to pray to him for deliverance when we face oppression from enemies.

Understanding the Word. Psalm 140 opens with the psalmist making a plea to the Lord for deliverance (vv. 1–3) and protection (vv. 4–5) from violent and evil foes. At the end of Psalm 139 (vv. 19–24), the psalmist was under pressure from the wicked. Psalm 140 follows with a lament that gives voice to the psalmist's need. The psalmist uses three images for the danger he feels. His opponents plot violent wars (v. 2), accuse him with tongues like snakes (v. 3), and have set traps for him (v. 5). In response, he turns to the Lord as the true source of security and hope (vv. 1, 4).

Verses 6–8 sit at the psalm's center and serve to articulate the psalmist's core faith in and allegiance to the Lord. The Lord is our God, our Lord, and our strong deliverer. The psalmist's sole hope for deliverance and help is the Lord, so he pleads for God to hear his prayer (v. 6) based on God's past faithfulness in protecting him (v. 7). Specifically, he requests that God stand against the evil plots and desires of his foes (v. 8).

In verses 9–11, the psalmist asks God for a reversal of fortune—that those who were slandering him and threatening him with violence would have their actions turned against them. In verse 9, he asks that their words may overwhelm them (cf. v. 3). In verse 10, he pleads that they fall into traps (cf. v. 5). In verse 11, he calls for his opponents to face uncertainty in their land (cf. v. 2). These verses help us articulate our prayers and invite us to be specific in our requests. There is no sugarcoating. The psalmist asks God for protection and specifically describes what that might look like. He is not taking matters into his own hands but releasing the outcome to the Lord in whom he trusts.

Verses 12–13 are a confession of the psalmist's trust in the Lord. This faith is rooted in God's commitment to the marginalized and poor (v. 12). This is central to the biblical faith. God is not merely for the powerful; God is for the neglected, hurting, weak, oppressed, and needy. This is good news. We don't have to make it on our own. When we are desperate for what only God can do, we stand in the shoes of the psalmist. Verse 13 widens the psalm to the community of all God's people and anticipates a time of thanksgiving.

1. How does Psalm 140 teach us to pray when we are under attack from those who intend to harm us?
2. What are the characteristics of the person who can pray Psalm 140 with integrity?

THREE

Psalm 144

Psalm 144 *Praise be to the Lord my Rock, who trains my hands for war, my fingers for battle.* [2]*He is my loving God and my fortress, my stronghold and my deliverer, my shield, in whom I take refuge, who subdues peoples under me.*

[3]Lord, what are human beings that you care for them, mere mortals that you think of them? [4]They are like a breath; their days are like a fleeting shadow.

[5]Part your heavens, Lord, and come down; touch the mountains, so that they smoke. [6]Send forth lightning and scatter the enemy; shoot your arrows and rout them. [7]Reach down your hand from on high; deliver me and rescue me from the mighty waters, from the hands of foreigners [8]whose mouths are full of lies, whose right hands are deceitful.

[9]I will sing a new song to you, my God; on the ten-stringed lyre I will make music to you, [10]to the One who gives victory to kings, who delivers his servant David.

From the deadly sword [11]deliver me; rescue me from the hands of foreigners whose mouths are full of lies, whose right hands are deceitful.

[12]Then our sons in their youth will be like well-nurtured plants, and our daughters will be like pillars carved to adorn a palace. [13]Our barns will be filled with every kind of provision. Our sheep will increase by thousands, by tens of thousands in our fields; [14]our oxen will draw heavy loads. There will be no breaching of walls, no going into captivity, no cry of distress in our streets. [15]Blessed is the people of whom this is true; blessed is the people whose God is the Lord.

Key Observation. Happy are the people whose God is the Lord because he is their true source of security and blessing.

Understanding the Word. Psalm 144 is a prayer by the king for God's people. It is the seventh of eight consecutive psalms attributed to David (138–145). This week we've read a psalm of thanksgiving (138) and lament (140). Laments dominate the middle portion of this block of Davidic psalms (138–143), but with Psalm 144 we find a psalm that anchors hope and security in the Lord. The language of this psalm is similar to phrases from earlier parts of the Psalter:

8:4 to 144:3
18:1, 2, 34, 46–47 to 144:1–2
18:9 to 144:5
18:14 to 144:6
18:16, 44–45 to 144:7–11
33:2–3 to 144:9
33:12 to 144:15

These references are significant because the Psalter ends with David echoing the songs of the past. This serves as a signal to God's people that the ancient ways are still the way forward. Hebrews 13:8 reminds us that "Jesus Christ is the same yesterday and today and forever."

There are two major sections in Psalm 144: a prayer by/for the king (vv. 1–11) and a concluding section of prayer and blessing for the community as a whole (vv. 12–15).

Psalm 144 opens with anchoring statements in verses 1–4. In verses 1–2, the psalmist praises the Lord, who is his source of security, by reciting a series of metaphors for the Lord: "rock," "fortress," "stronghold," "deliverer," "shield," and "refuge." Notice the repeated use of "my" with these words. This is a powerful reminder that faith begins with the individual. Here the king proclaims dependence on the Lord alone for *personal* security. The greatest danger to one's faith in the Lord is to trust oneself or another for security. Verses 3–4 remind us of the finite power of humans. Unlike the "rock" and "fortress," humans are "a breath" and a "fleeting shadow."

In verses 5–8, the king prays to God for protection and deliverance from enemies. These verses use the cosmic language of creation to portray the power of the Lord over the heavens and the earth, as well as the king's adversaries. The Lord is infinitely mightier than any threat facing his people.

Verses 9–11 envision a full deliverance followed by praise and worship. In this prayer, the king does not request human strength or weaponry. Instead, his focus is on the Lord as the One who saves. All the king does is express an intention to worship God for the victory he will provide.

Psalm 144 ends with a prayer for security and abundance for all God's people. The model prayer includes petitions for the psalmist, but also extends these to others. Verse 15 is a fundamental statement of faith for God's people: it is a state of blessedness to be in relationship with the Lord.

1. Which of the metaphors for the Lord is this psalm do you find most reassuring? Why?

2. How does Psalm 144 describe happiness? In what ways have you experienced a state of happiness rooted in your relationship with the Lord?

FOUR

Psalm 145

Psalm 145 NRSV *I will extol you, my God and King, and bless your name forever and ever. [2]Every day I will bless you, and praise your name forever and ever. [3]Great is the LORD, and greatly to be praised; his greatness is unsearchable.*

[4]One generation shall laud your works to another, and shall declare your mighty acts. [5]On the glorious splendor of your majesty, and on your wondrous works, I will meditate. [6]The might of your awesome deeds shall be proclaimed, and I will declare your greatness. [7]They shall celebrate the fame of your abundant goodness, and shall sing aloud of your righteousness.

[8]The LORD is gracious and merciful, slow to anger and abounding in steadfast love. [9]The LORD is good to all, and his compassion is over all that he has made.

[10]All your works shall give thanks to you, O LORD, and all your faithful shall bless you. [11]They shall speak of the glory of your kingdom, and tell of your power, [12]to make known to all people your mighty deeds, and the glorious splendor of your kingdom. [13]Your kingdom is an everlasting kingdom, and your dominion endures throughout all generations.

The LORD is faithful in all his words, and gracious in all his deeds. [14]The LORD upholds all who are falling, and raises up all who are bowed down. [15]The eyes of all look to you, and you give them their food in due season. [16]You open your hand, satisfying the desire of every living thing. [17]The LORD is just in all his ways, and kind in all his doings. [18]The LORD is near to all who call on him, to all who call on him in truth. [19]He fulfills the desire of all who fear him; he also hears their cry, and saves them. [20]The LORD watches over all who love him, but all the wicked he will destroy.

[21]My mouth will speak the praise of the LORD, and all flesh will bless his holy name forever and ever.

Key Observation. We praise the Lord because of his gracious, faithful, merciful love, and in order to make him known to all people.

Understanding the Word. Psalm 145 brings the final block of Davidic psalms to a rousing conclusion. It is audacious and dynamic in its praise. David packs all his emotions and deep faith in the Lord into these twenty-one verses. This psalm offers a model witness of how to declare and describe the greatness of God. The totality of its message is implied by its acrostic structure (see the introduction to Psalms 111–112 for an explanation of acrostic psalms). Jewish tradition called for believers to recite Psalm 145 three times a day.

Every verse of Psalm 145 resounds in worship of the Lord for who he is and what he has done. Verse 1 sets the tone by setting the Lord apart as "God and King." This is significant. We constantly face the temptation of substituting a person, belief system, ideology, or object for the true security of the Lord. David reminds us that even Israel's greatest king served the true King and worshipped him extravagantly. Only the Lord is worthy of praise because of his great deeds (vv. 4–7).

The Lord's mighty acts of salvation find their roots in God's loving character. Verses 8–9 recite and apply Exodus 34:6–7 by emphasizing the centrality of the Lord's gracious, faithful, merciful love. God's love is infinite and extends to all creation. It manifests itself ultimately in the sending of Jesus Christ the Son into the world.

What is the proper response to the infinite love of the Lord? It is worship with a purpose. Verses 10–13a portray the praise of God as a testimony to those who do not yet know of his greatness. David reminds us of the core truth that the gospel comes to us on its way to someone else and to someplace else. The experience of God's kingdom is a message to be *shared*. God's kingdom is forever. It is the hope of all the earth. It is no coincidence that Jesus will begin his earthly ministry announcing the kingdom/reign of God (Matthew 4:17; Mark 1:15; and Luke 4:16–21).

Verses 13b–20 lay out the true benefits of living under the dynamic reign of the Lord. These verses acknowledge the difficulty of life, but proclaim a dependence on God's faithfulness and graciousness to supply all needs. Verse 20 starkly contrasts two approaches to life: God guards those who love him, but those who are wicked face destruction. Psalm 1:6 opened the Psalter with a similar message.

Verse 21 concludes the psalm with David again declaring his intention to praise the Lord. He also envisions a scene where all living beings worship God's name forever. This verse sets the stage for the grand climax of the Psalter (Psalms 146–150) in which all creation gathers to worship the Lord.

1. How have you experienced the Lord's faithful, gracious, and merciful love?
2. How have your experiences of grace created opportunities to share this good news with others?

FIVE

Psalms 146–150

Psalm 150:6 NRSV *Let everything that breathes praise the* Lord*! Praise the Lord!*

Key Observation. The book of Psalms serves as a prayer book for God's missional people. The final word is a vision of the successful completion of God's mission in which all creation joins together in praise of the Lord.

Understanding the Word. Psalms 146–150 bring the Psalter to a resounding climax, with all creation praising the Lord. These five psalms serve as a concluding doxology that remind us that the end of our journey is the praise of the Lord for who he is and what he has done. This is the testimony of God's missional people to the world.

We've read the Psalms as a book of prayers for God's people on mission. As followers of Jesus, we live in light of Jesus' fulfillment of God's original call to Israel to be the agents of his blessings to the world (Genesis 12:3; Exodus 19:5–6; Isaiah 42:6; 49:6). As God's people, we live as witnesses to the good news of his grace for the sake of all people (1 Peter 2:9; Matthew 28:18–20; Acts 1:8). As we follow Jesus into the world on God's mission, we are not immune from hardship and challenges. As we've read through the Psalms, we've experienced the highs and lows of the life of faith.

Psalms 1–2 opened the Psalter by describing the "happy" or "blessed" life as one shaped by Scripture and by the security found in the Lord's reign through the Messiah. These themes continue throughout the Psalter. In Psalms 90–100, we see the theme of security particularly emphasized. These psalms pointed to a renewed future for God's post-exile people through trust in the Lord as King. Psalm 119 showed us that the Psalter's foundational commitment to a life of faithfulness is rooted in Scripture.

The majority of Books I–III are laments that cried out to God for help in the face of life's difficulties. These play a critical role in shaping us as God's missional people. Living as a witness to the world means that our need for prayer in all circumstances will increase because we will face enemies, illness, national emergencies, and even times of despair. But the Psalms give us prayers for all occasions and provide our lips with a vocabulary for honest interaction with God. In Book V, Psalm 130:1 captured the essence of lament for us: "Out of the depths I cry to you, LORD."

Books IV and V also emphasize the presence of God's steadfast love (*hesed*) throughout Israel's history. This is the faithful love and mercy of God that forms our story as his people. God's *hesed* is the final word, making sense of our history and inviting us to give thanks for our salvation (Psalms 104–107 and 136). For the Israelites, the exodus and gift of the promised land served as the principal acts of salvation (Psalms 113–118). We rejoice in the life, death, and resurrection of Jesus.

By ending the Psalter with all creation in praise, Psalms 146–150 audaciously declare the victory of God. As God's witnesses today, we live as a people of faith, hope, and love in the confidence of a beautiful and secure future. Let us join together now in praise of the Lord in anticipation of a future day when *all* will join us (Philippians 2:9–11).

1. What has your study of the Psalms taught you about prayer?
2. What roles do lament, thanksgiving, and praise serve in your life?

WEEK EIGHT

GATHERING DISCUSSION OUTLINE

A. Open session in prayer. Ask that God would astonish us anew with fresh insight from God's Word and transform us into the disciples that Jesus desires us to become.

B. View the video for this week's readings.

C. What were key insights or takeaways that you gained from your reading during the week and from watching the video commentary? In particular, how did these help you to grow in your faith and understanding of Scripture this week? What parts of the Bible lesson or study raised questions for you?

D. Discuss questions selected from the daily readings.

1. **KEY OBSERVATION:** God's steadfast love is the reason for giving thanks to him and testifying of his faithfulness before the nations.

   DISCUSSION QUESTION: How does Psalm 138 teach us to give thanks when we find ourselves in the midst of a world that doesn't yet know Jesus as Lord?

2. **KEY OBSERVATION:** The Lord invites us to pray to him for deliverance when we face oppression from enemies.

   DISCUSSION QUESTION: How does Psalm 140 teach us to pray when we are under attack from those who intend to harm us?

3. **KEY OBSERVATION:** Happy are the people whose God is the Lord because he is their true source of security and blessing.

   DISCUSSION QUESTION: How does Psalm 144 describe happiness? In what ways have you experienced a state of happiness rooted in your relationship with the Lord?

4. **KEY OBSERVATION:** We praise the Lord because of his gracious, faithful, merciful love, and in order to make him known to all people.

   DISCUSSION QUESTION: How have you experienced the Lord's faithful, gracious, and merciful love?

5. **KEY OBSERVATION:** The book of Psalms serves as a prayer book for God's missional people. The final word is a vision of the successful completion of God's mission in which all creation joins together in praise of the Lord.

   DISCUSSION QUESTION: What has your study of the Psalms taught you about prayer?

E. As the study concludes, consider specific ways that this week's Bible lesson invites you to grow and calls you to change. How do this week's psalms teach us to pray? How do they call us to think differently? How do they challenge us to change in order to align ourselves with God's work in the world? What specific actions should we take to apply the insights of the lesson into our daily lives? What kind of person does our Bible lesson call us to become?

F. Close session with prayer. Emphasize God's ongoing work of transformation in our lives in preparation for loving mission and service in the world. Pray for missing class members as well as for persons whom we need to invite to join our study.

www.ingramcontent.com/pod-product-compliance
Ingram Content Group UK Ltd.
Pitfield, Milton Keynes, MK11 3LW, UK
UKHW021401070726
13610UKWH00012B/68

9 781628 245783